Academic Librarianship
Past, Present, and Future

Academic Librarianship
Past, Present, and Future
A Festschrift in Honor of David Kaser

Edited by
John Richardson, Jr.
and
Jinnie Y. Davis

1989
Libraries Unlimited, Inc. • Englewood, Colorado

Z
675
.U5
A317
1989

Copyright © 1989 John V. Richardson, Jr. and Jinnie Y. Davis
All Rights Reserved
Printed in the United States of America

No part of this publication may be reproduced, stored in a retrieval system, or transmitted, in any form or by any means, electronic, mechanical, photocopying, recording, or otherwise without the prior written permission of the publisher.

LIBRARIES UNLIMITED, INC.
P.O. Box 3988
Englewood, Colorado 80155-3988

Library of Congress Cataloging-in-Publication Data

Academic librarianship, past, present, and future : a festschrift in
  honor of David Kaser / edited by John Richardson, Jr. and Jinnie Y.
  Davis.
  xvi, 175 p. 17x25 cm.
    ISBN 0-87287-669-1
    1. Libraries, University and college. 2. Kaser, David, 1924-   .
  I. Kaser, David, 1924-   . II. Richardson, John V., 1949-   .
  III. Davis, Jinnie Y.
  Z675.U5A317 1989
  027.7--dc20   89-12143
                                                                   CIP

Contents

Preface xi

Foreword xiii
    Edward G. Holley

Part I
The Future of Academic Librarianship

1 – Librarianship and the CLR, 1969-1987 3
    Warren J. Haas
    Overview 3
    Observations 8
    Notes 12

2 – The Influence of Computer Technology on Academic Library Buildings: A Slice of Recent History 13
    Philip D. Leighton and David C. Weber
    The 1960s and 1970s 14
    The 1980s 18
    The 1990s 23
    Notes 28

3 – Retrieval of Information from Computerized Book Texts 31
    Frederick G. Kilgour
    System Purpose and Design 33
    Database Construction 34
    Research and Development 35
    Benefits of Mature EIDOS 38
    Notes 38

Part II
The Present Situation of Academic Librarianship

4 – Verner Clapp and Preservation of Library Materials: The
   Years at the Council on Library Resources............................43
   William J. Crowe
   Beginnings at the CLR..44
   First Work with Barrow: Adding to Knowledge and Mobilizing Interest...46
   Stalemate in the ALA Committee on Permanent/Durable Paper..........49
   The ARL Committee: Beginnings at Cooperation......................51
   The Library Technology Project and Library Binding.................52
   Preservation Microfilming – Emphasis on Bibliographic Control..........53
   Looking to the Future: Institutionalizing Change.....................55
   The Last Years – Research and Exhortation..........................56
   Conclusions...60
   Notes..61

5 – Faculty Status of Librarians: A Comparative Study of Two
   Universities in the United Kingdom and How They Compare to the
   Association of College and Research Libraries Standards...............67
   James L. Mullins
   Literature Review...68
   Case Studies...69
   Criteria..71
   Conclusions...75
   Notes..77

Part III
A Historical Examination of Academic Librarianship

6 – The College Library Section, 1889-1923: Predecessor to the
   Association of College and Research Libraries........................81
   Charles E. Hale
   A Perspicacious Beginning: ACRL, 1889-1923.........................81
   Membership and Organizational Concerns.............................84
   Reference Librarians and Reorganization.............................86
   Sectional Programs and Selected Activities, 1889-1923.................87
   The Section's First Constitution: 1923..............................91
   Summary..93
   Notes..95

7 – An Uncertain Crusade: The History of Library Use Instruction
   in a Changing Educational Environment..............................97
   Larry Hardesty and John Mark Tucker
   Justin Winsor and the Early Years: 1880-1900........................97
   Bureaucracy, Experimentation, and Philanthropy 1901-1940............100
   Bricks, Books, and the Search for Identity 1941-1968.................102

A Grassroots Movement and Growing Sophistication 1969-1980s.......104
Conclusion 105
Notes 107

Part IV
Kaser and His Contributions to Librarianship

8 – David Kaser and Sino-American Librarianship......................115
    Margaret C. Fung
First Phase of Sino-American Library Activity.......................115
Kaser's Involvement in the Second Phase............................117
Conclusion 124
Notes 125
Additional Readings..128

9 – David Kaser: A Biographical Sketch...............................129
    Joanne E. Passet
The Early Years..129
The Middle Years...130
Summary of Honors and Achievements.............................131

Appendixes

    A. A David Kaser Chronology.................................135
    B. A Chronology of Publications by David Kaser................139
    C. Doctoral Students Supervised by David Kaser................151
    D. Building and Space Consultancies of David Kaser.............155

Contributors 165

Index 167

Preface

This festschrift honors David Kaser upon his sixty-fifth birthday and celebrates a life of distinction in scholarship, education, and humanity. As doctoral students working with Dr. Kaser on our dissertations at Indiana University, we talked about the possibility of showing our gratitude to him through the creation of such a volume. A decade later, our dream has become a reality.

Royalties from this volume will be donated to Indiana University's School of Library and Information Science where a scholarship has been established in David Kaser's name. This fund will be used to attract highly qualified students in the two areas of David Kaser's own interests: academic librarianship and library history. Anyone wishing to make contributions should inquire first of the Dean, School of Library and Information Science, Indiana University, Bloomington, IN 47405.

We have organized this volume to reflect the scholarly interests of David Kaser. The first three chapters suggest the future of academic librarianship. The next two chapters critically examine the existing situation. In the third section, the chapter authors reveal history in the service of the present and explore how academic librarianship came of age. The final section and the four appendixes trace the development of David Kaser's career.

We wish to thank all of the authors who have contributed their time and efforts to this festschrift. And we join them in dedicating this volume to David Kaser—*totus, teres, atque rotundus.*

John Richardson, Jr.
Associate Professor
Graduate School of Library and Information Science
UCLA

Jinnie Y. Davis
Assistant to the Director for Planning and Development
North Carolina State University Libraries

Foreword

When I began to prepare this foreword to David Kaser's festschrift, he and I had just finished an evaluation of a proposed doctoral program at the School of Information and Library Studies of the State University of New York (SUNY) at Buffalo. Kaser left soon thereafter for Taipei where he consulted on a new library building for National Taiwan University. At the same time he continued working on his history of academic library buildings in the United States, a book which will undoubtedly become the definitive study of that topic.

These three projects—evaluating a proposed new doctoral program, helping a university abroad with a new library building, and continuing his research into our professional history—are indicative of the contributions Kaser has made to his chosen profession. His work has been solidly grounded in book and library history. His educational work reflects almost two decades as a faculty member at one of the leading schools of library/information science in the United States. And his building consulting embodies what he learned from two decades as a consultant and as staff member/director at Ball State, Washington University (St. Louis), Vanderbilt, and Cornell.

David Kaser's learning has never stopped. An early advocate of the latest modern management principles in libraries, he has kept up in this field as well as in the area of library technology. He is more adept at teaching telecourses and using personal computers and other developing technology than most faculty members and library directors. In his long love affair with the history of books, libraries, and printing, David Kaser has demonstrated that he is no stodgy historian. His articles, books, and speeches are replete with wonderful bits of humor. That he is well respected by other historians was attested by his election to membership in the prestigious American Antiquarian Society.

CONTRIBUTORS

The authors of the essays in this festschrift include both distinguished colleagues and former Kaser students who are beginning to make their own mark on our profession. In the former category is *Warren J. Haas*, president of the Council on Library Resources (CLR), who reflects on two decades of the council's efforts to improve academic/research librarianship. Under Haas's leadership, the council changed direction significantly. His essay provides a graphic picture of the council's emphasis upon specialized training, professional education, and research librarianship. In view of the recent evaluation of CLR and the board's decision to continue its work, Haas's overview of the past two decades and his questions about the future are well worth consideration.

Also among this group of distinguished seniors are *David C. Weber* and *Philip D. Leighton*, whose revision of Keyes Metcalf's *Planning Academic and Research Library Buildings* (Chicago: American Library Association, 1986), is a major contribution to library literature. Appropriately, they provide an important paper on computer technology's influence on academic library buildings. One can safely predict that their excellent review of where we have been and where we may be going in technology and library buildings will become an article often read and quoted by both practicing librarians and students.

When *Frederick G. Kilgour* assumed the presidency of the Ohio College Library Center (OCLC) in 1967 he already had a demonstrated record of achievement in bibliographical activity. Yet, despite great hope for technology in the early 1960s, the profession had become discouraged at the number of failures to use technology successfully in libraries. Within five years Kilgour not only had put together an impressive organization in Columbus but also had librarians in other parts of the country knocking on his door. Thus when OCLC, Inc., celebrated its twentieth birthday in 1987, the restructured organization had expanded its services not only to other libraries throughout the country, but also to libraries in Western Europe and the Far East. He is truly among the pioneers of information science and technology, as the American Society for Information Science designated him at its fiftieth anniversary conference last year. Now retired from the nation's major bibliographic utility, Kilgour continues his examination of the next stage of technological development: computerized book texts. His paper provides an overview of EIDOS, "an interactive, online method for retrieving information from written books that are in digital form." Kilgour's efforts to reduce the high failure rate of librarians in answering user's questions have led him to concentrate his attention on this problem area. He expresses optimism that EIDOS will not only increase the success rate of librarians in responding to reference queries but also reduce costs.

Next come the Kaser students.

William J. Crowe traces Verner Clapp's role as a leader in support of early library preservation efforts. Clapp, as the first president of the Council on Library Resources, gave strong support to William J. Barrows's study of book paper deterioration. Crowe provides an interesting glimpse into the Clapp-Barrows collaboration, which had such significant consequences for development of acid-free paper.

Faculty status for academic librarians has been debated with heat and occasional flashes of light for the last forty years. *James L. Mullins* gives a new twist to the perennial debate with his comparison of the situation in the United States and the United Kingdom. There are more similarities between privileges and responsibilities among the librarians than one might guess, despite differences in higher education patterns in the two countries. That this issue still concerns American academic librarians and will continue to be debated is clear from ACRL's recently published *Academic Status: Statements and Resources* (1988).

Charles E. Hale, from his dissertation under Kaser, provides a look at the College Library Section of the American Library Association (ALA) for the period of 1889 to 1923. His essay is especially timely since the College Library Section's successor organization, the Association of College and Research Libraries (ACRL), will celebrate the centennial of academic librarians in ALA as well as its own fiftieth anniversary at its national conference in Cincinnati on April 5-8, 1989. Hale's piece is also appropriate for this festschrift since David Kaser has had a major role in ACRL, having served as editor of *College and Research Libraries*, 1963-1969, and as ACRL president, 1968-1969.

Larry Hardesty and *John Mark Tucker* provide an intriguing essay on one of the major topics of the last decade: library use instruction, more familiarly known as bibliographic instruction. Their tracing of the history of this "uncertain crusade" may well be one of the finest pieces yet to appear on this topic. User education has indeed waxed and waned over the past century. With the recent efforts at undergraduate curricula reform, which the authors address in the historical context, librarians may have an opportunity to enter a golden period of user instruction. Hardesty and Tucker's history and suggestions about the future are well worth pondering, especially among devotees of bibliographic instruction.

Margaret C. Fung adds the only sketch on Kaser's extensive work for librarianship abroad with her essay on his influence on Sino-American librarianship—an impact that continues, as the earlier paragraphs in this foreword have noted. Kaser's influence on Chinese librarianship has now extended over two decades. American librarians are probably most familiar with his *Book Pirating in Taiwan*, published by the University of Pennsylvania Press in 1969. Kaser's work has been described by Hsiun Tun-Sheng, president of the Chung Hwa Book Company, as having led the Chinese government and Chinese academicians "to understand that the protection of intellectual property is essential to the nation's development." Fung notes that Kaser, in his extensive efforts in support of Sino-American librarianship, has always emphasized the importance of "adaptation" rather than "adoption" of "library practices when they are introduced from one country to another." She applauds the sensitivity of David Kaser in working with librarians in the international arena.

Joanne E. Passet's biographical sketch of David Kaser is followed by appendixes that include *Jinnie Davis*'s list of Kaser's publications and *John Richardson*'s list of Kaser's doctoral students and their dissertations, plus a list of Kaser's building and space consultancies. This is truly a remarkable record for any person.

When David Kaser left Cornell in 1973, he said he was going to Indiana because for four years administrative pressures had prevented him from writing a book. That may have been a slight exaggeration. After all, two of his books, *Book Pirating in Taiwan* and *Library Development in Eight Asian Countries* appeared the year after he became director at Cornell (1969). No matter. His years as a teacher, adviser, consultant, researcher, and writer have been incredibly productive. Books and articles from Bloomington have followed, notably *Books for a Sixpence* (1980) and *Books in Camp and Battle* (1984). In 1986 Indiana University recognized his research and professional contributions by naming him a University Distinguished Professor, an accolade given rarely in Bloomington or in any other major research university.

As we read these papers and learn more about our profession—its past, its present, and its future—we can only be grateful for David Kaser's many contributions. And we will congratulate Kaser's colleagues and students, the editors, the essayists, and the publisher for providing us with this informative volume.

Edward G. Holley
Professor
School of Information and Library Science
The University of North Carolina at Chapel Hill

Part I
THE FUTURE OF ACADEMIC LIBRARIANSHIP

1
Librarianship and the CLR, 1969-1987

Warren J. Haas

The Council on Library Resources (CLR) was established in 1956 by the Ford Foundation "to aid in the solution of library problems." That simple mandate has taken CLR along many complex but interesting paths during more than thirty years, and none has been more challenging than the one exploring the profession itself. This paper is a historical review of CLR activities concerned with librarianship. It is not a definitive survey of the state of the profession, but rather a personal reflection on the efforts and the influence of one organization that has sought to help academic and research librarians understand fully and prepare to meet the responsibilities of their profession.

OVERVIEW

Even though the CLR's *Second Annual Report* noted that "it is probable that the outstanding problem of library work at the moment, as viewed by librarians themselves, arises from difficulties in recruiting adequately trained staffs," there was no significant program activity in this arena until 1969, in the council's thirteenth year. During the following eighteen years, through 1987, nearly $5.2 million in grants were awarded in the broad area of librarianship, in all about 10.9 percent of total CLR program expenditures since 1956. There has been a pronounced shift in emphasis, from negligible expenditures during the early years of the council's history to 21 percent of total program costs during the most recent three-year period, 1985-1987.

With the exception of fifteen to twenty grants for a variety of nonrecurring projects or events, funding for professional programs has been concentrated in three areas: (1) grants to individuals for research or advanced study, (2) grants to organizations or institutions to provide specialized training for individual librarians, and (3) grants to library schools to improve or expand professional education programs.

Initially, the emphasis was on research, advanced study, and specialized training for individuals; professional education, generally, and library schools, specifically, received little attention. Beginning in 1980, a thorough review of council-funded activities for librarians was undertaken and a new program, Professional Education and Training for Research Librarianship (PETREL), was formed with financial support from the Andrew W. Mellon Foundation and the Carnegie Corporation of New York. An advisory committee was established to help shape program directions and to review proposals. In addition to endorsing CLR support for research and specialized training, the advisory committee encouraged the CLR to work directly with library schools, both to promote development of new programs pertinent to research library needs and to urge evaluation of current instructional programs. The Pew Memorial Trust provided support for much of this new element of the CLR program.

The continuing CLR projects supporting librarianship from 1969 to the present are identified in table 1.1 and are described in the next section.

Research and Advanced Study

Librarians have fewer opportunities than do individuals in many other professions to obtain support for research. To promote analytical studies and to encourage work by librarians, CLR has funded three competitive programs during the past eighteen years that, together, have aided more than 400 individuals. The CLR Fellowship Program (1969-1979) provided awards for research to librarians for use over periods of three to twelve months to cover research-related expenses while the Fellows were on leave with pay (a program requirement) from their home institutions. Two-thirds of the awards (141 of 218) were made during the first six years of the program. A decline in the number of applications prompted a program review, and in 1983 a new version of the Fellowship Program, the Cooperative Research program, was designed to stimulate research by promoting collaboration between librarians and research faculty members. During the past five years, more than 200 proposals have been submitted and seventy-nine grants made through the Cooperative Research program. As with the original Fellowship Program, funds are for incremental costs and not for salaries of investigators. A large number of publications, many of them listed in CLR annual reports, have stemmed from the research grants, and many past grantees are among the most active members of the profession.

The third effort in this group, an experimental Advanced Study Program designed to enable librarians to concentrate full-time for one year on an academic discipline, was sponsored by CLR during 1975-1977. Nine librarians received financial support equivalent to salary plus tuition.

Table 1.1.
Librarianship and CLR, 1969-1987: program summary

	1970	1975	1980	1985
Research, advanced study				
Fellowships (218) 1969-79 $630,000	——————————————			
Advanced Study Program (9 students) 1975-77 $185,000		—		
Cooperative Research grants (79) 1983- approx. $200,000				— — — —
Specialized training				
ARL Office of Management Studies 1969-83 $773,000	————————————————————			
Management Intern Program (47 interns) 1974- $1,439,000		————————————————— — — —		
Health Sciences Intern Program (9 interns) 1978-80 $298,000			—	
UCLA Senior Fellows (58 fellows) 1982, '83, '85, '87 $260,000				——— — — —
ARL Institutes for Library Educators (3) 1984, '86, '88 $145,000				—— — —
Internships for Recent Graduates (5 programs) 1985- $276,000				—— — —
Professional education				
Chicago/MLS for Ph.D.s (9 students) 1974-76 $103,000		—		
Chicago/library management 1981 $104,000			—	
Michigan/research librarianship 1981-83 $325,000			—	
Frontiers Conferences (2) 1981, 1983 $123,000			—	
Planning grants (15) 1984-85 $65,400				—
Implementation grants (3) 1985-86 $200,000				—

Specialized Training

The past two decades have transformed the setting and conditions in which future research librarians will do their work. Organizationally, economically, and technologically, the changes are dramatic, far-reaching, and demanding. By and large, those who must reshape libraries and those who will be responsible for library performance into the twenty-first century are now working in libraries. It follows that today's librarians will need new skills and expanded capabilities if they are to succeed in the new operating setting. In recognition of this fact, CLR has, since 1969, funded five programs, each designed to provide specialized training for librarians.

Measured in terms of continuity and costs, the Academic Library Management Intern Program (along with a parallel program for health sciences librarians, 1978-1980) is the most prominent of CLR-managed activities. Offered annually since 1974 (with an occasional one-year interlude), the program has attracted 603 applicants. Internships have been awarded to forty-seven librarians.

A second and remarkably effective program has been that undertaken by the Office of Management Studies (OMS) of the Association of Research Libraries (ARL). Council funds and guidance through the early years of OMS helped to establish an imaginative and influential set of specialized training programs and an extensive series of publications pertinent to all aspects of library operations. CLR funding for OMS was continued in diminishing amounts for almost fifteen years, until the OMS became self-supporting through budgeted ARL funds, project-specific grants from other sources, and income-generating activities.

Three additional CLR activities, all developed in the context of the PETREL program, are each focused on a particular group of librarians. An intensive three-week program on management methods for academic library directors and senior administrators has been developed and offered, currently in alternate years, by the Graduate School of Library and Information Science at the University of California at Los Angeles (UCLA). A second program, operated by the ARL/OMS, is designed for faculty members of accredited library schools and is intended to provide detailed current information about the issues and problems affecting academic research library operations. The third program is intended to explore and demonstrate ways to help recent graduates of library schools maintain academic momentum and build on their personal interests during the first years of professional practice. The university libraries that have established these Internships for Recent Graduates are providing an opportunity for staff members to apply their professional learning to librarywide issues, thus avoiding some of the constraints generated by exclusive and premature concentration on the demands of a specific position.

Professional Education

With the exception of providing support for an experimental program (1974-1976) intended to encourage individuals holding doctoral degrees in a subject field to pursue a professional degree in library science at the University of Chicago, CLR was not much involved in professional education until several PETREL-sponsored activities were developed. Two conferences, one sponsored by UCLA and the other by the University of British Columbia, explored, first, the characteristics of the setting in which academic libraries would function in the future and, second, the projected influence of technology on library school curricula. These discussions and the resulting publications[1] helped set the stage for program development.

A second PETREL-sponsored effort involved support for new and specialized academic programs in two library schools. The first, a certificate program at the University of Chicago, combined coursework in both the Graduate School of Management and the Graduate Library School. Six librarians, all with professional degrees and several years of experience, completed the program in the first year. The program was canceled because subsequently there were too few successful applicants.

The University of Michigan, in a second experimental undertaking, established a two-year program for a limited number of students seeking a concentration in research librarianship. In addition to completing an expanded academic program, students served a three-month internship in a research library. The program continued for three years with CLR support, was extended with assistance from other sources, and continues today in modified form as the University Library Associates Program, established in 1985, also with CLR funding.

Finally, and again following consultation with the PETREL advisory committee, the CLR offered planning grants to accredited library schools to encourage an analysis of such topics as student needs, interests, and career paths, with the goal of supplementing and refining the academic programs offered in the field of academic librarianship. Fifteen schools undertook and completed planning efforts of widely varying kinds. Subsequently, three of these library schools were funded to implement new programs: the University of Wisconsin, for a certificate program in research design and methods; the University of Chicago, for a new curriculum concentration in library automation and information systems; and Louisiana State University, for a multidisciplinary curriculum for library systems analysts.

In addition to those multiyear programs, CLR has funded a number of individual projects. These include salary surveys, a demographic study of the profession, continuing education conferences, and preparation of a bibliography of works on librarianship. The details of these and other projects are included in various CLR annual reports.

OBSERVATIONS

Programs for Individuals

CLR follows a specified and thorough review process in assessing grant applications. Proposals from individuals (for fellowships and internships) receive written evaluations from appropriate CLR staff members and, for the most promising prospects, an evaluation by external reviewers, usually working together as a team for each program cycle. In the case of the Management Interns, finalists are interviewed. When a university or organization is funded to operate a program, the institution assumes responsibility for selecting participants. CLR-managed programs, before they are begun, undergo similar scrutiny, often by advisory committees (PETREL is the pertinent example) and by the CLR board.

Performance reviews generally are less structured than reviews of grant applications in all CLR-funded activities, but in the specific area of librarianship, several format evaluations have been done and evidence of several kinds is available. For example, each CLR annual report lists publications stemming from funded activity; over the years, the number and quality of such publications has been, and continues to be, impressive.

A formal review of the Management Intern Program was completed in 1982. Almost all past interns and their hosts were interviewed, program benefits were enumerated, and subsequent career paths of the interns were traced. Several suggestions to improve program operation were offered and some were subsequently adopted. The program received overall high marks in 1982, and continues to be well regarded, but the difficulties inherent from the beginning persist. The number of applicants fluctuates widely, but has tended downwards (twenty-one in 1987, for the 1988-1989 intern year). It is evident that a majority of eligible librarians find it impossible to contemplate taking leave from their positions for nine months, principally because of professional or personal responsibilities. There is no evidence that financial considerations are of consequence, because the stipend is typically close to actual salaries and, in every case, modest differentials have been met by the home institutions.

The Senior Fellows program, which now lasts three weeks, creates no such problem. While the program is one of CLR's more recent enterprises, a method for formal assessment has been developed and put in place. The career records of the first two classes of UCLA Senior Fellows have been compared to those of a control group, and interesting differences in characteristics have been identified.[2] The study will be repeated after an appropriate interval, both to test initial findings and to help establish changes in career characteristics over time. As with the CLR Management Interns, most Senior Fellows give the program high marks.

An assessment method has been incorporated into most of the ALR/OMS programs over the years, again with generally positive responses and useful observations that have served to help refine many specific activities.

All in all, and as might be expected for activities that are selective and that provide financial support, there are strong personal endorsements. Within CLR, there is a strong conviction that most program components concentrating on individuals, whether supporting research or specialized training, have been beneficial to many and of value to the profession at large.

Even so, important matters still need attention. Most libraries have not yet institutionalized a research leave program. Until this is done, neither research nor the profession is likely to flourish fully in academic settings. It is still uncommon for libraries to provide even partial financial support for individuals seeking to add substantively to specialized skills, despite the fact that, at this particular time, such skills are essential to improving library performance. Most important, there are still too few librarians who have built into their own professional lives a continuing commitment to purposeful professional growth. There has been progress in this direction, but the necessary critical mass has not yet been attained to imbed formal research and the enhancement of specialized skills in the basic definition of the profession. In short, this is an exceptional time for libraries and librarians, but the exceptional efforts required by each to meet the needs of the times are not yet fully formed.

Professional Education

Library school deans are as intensely concerned about the quality and nature of professional education as are many librarians. This is the most obvious and perhaps the least useful observation stemming from CLR's recent and fragmentary efforts in the arena of professional education. Moving from concern to effective action has proven to be difficult—for numerous, frequently noted, and sometimes valid reasons. For each academic program that is doing well, there are many others that are routine or intellectually dormant. CLR funding for analytical studies of and innovation in academic programs has not stimulated any broadly based evolution of librarianship as a profession or of professional library education by either librarians or library educators.

But the centrality of librarian-related issues to the future performance of libraries cannot be ignored, and dealing with those issues should not be deferred. The CLR continues to seek ways to be useful and is committed to the cause of librarianship over the long term. About twenty library directors and library school deans joined several members of the CLR staff and board at Wye Plantation, Maryland, in November 1986 to consider the topic "Information Studies, the Information Professions, and Research Library Leadership." There is not space here to record the full range of that discussion or that of the CLR board of directors a week or two later. But four matters that affect all aspects of librarianship—both operations and education—surfaced as the ones most in need of attention in any prescription for action.

1. *The shortage of first-rate candidates for faculty positions in library schools*

    Several deans, especially those new in their posts and trying to strengthen their schools, have reported difficulty in identifying individuals with distinctive research and publication records who would be viewed as fully credible academic appointments in the context of overall university standards and expectations for faculty generally. Further, it is exceptionally difficult to interest strong prospects from complementary disciplines in a career in library education.

2. *The low visibility of librarianship and library professional education*

Justified or not, the profession is handicapped by its image—tradition-bound and conservative, driven by internal operations, reactive rather than entrepreneurial, and having no clearly exclusive professional turf. Library schools themselves tend to be small in enrollment and faculty size, and they often have a marginal presence in the university. Salaries of librarians are low by most professional measures, thus constraining investment by individuals in their own primary and continuing professional education. For many of the same reasons, opportunities are limited for the wide-ranging and distinctive supplementary education that seems essential for a professional seeking to cope in a rapidly changing and demanding new operating setting.

3. *Ambiguity in the definition of "libraries" and "librarianship"*

The recent modification in the designation of many library schools by insertion of the term "information science" in one form or another is indicative of an attitude that assigns responsibility for past practices to librarians and aspirations for the future to a new and different breed. Extension of library school interests into pertinent new areas at times runs afoul of competing interests in business schools, computer science departments, schools of engineering, communication programs, and law schools. In universities, operating responsibility for information systems and services is frequently divided between libraries and computing centers; increasingly, the fragmentation is viewed as a bothersome problem to be solved administratively by superimposing a new position on what already exists. The failure to address the matters of substance behind this ambiguity sets limits on the development of librarianship and curtails constructive change in the underlying educational structure.

4. *The paucity of sound research on many important topics and the lack of a significant research tradition on which to build*

Even after acknowledging the production of many analytical studies over the years and the contributions of a few distinguished educators, the fact remains that the general quality of past and present research pertinent to the new information world does not match in scope, quality, or quantity reasonable expectations for an important field. CLR, with funds available for research in several broad areas, is handicapped by a shortage of proposals that justify support. Public and institutional policy questions, as distinct from technical topics, are of great importance but receive little rigorous attention. Measured against work done in other fields, library research does not provide a sufficient foundation for professional education or library management.[3]

If these are among the primary shortcomings that need attention, the matter of how to proceed remains. Recognizing that CLR can at best only stimulate other organizations and individuals to join in the search, the council is concentrating on three questions that may help point the way to future constructive action.

1. How can information studies be better described and more widely understood as a discrete and significant academic discipline? Unless the discipline is one of substantial and distinctive content, and is seen as such, professional education, which rests on the substance of the discipline, will continue to be concerned more with techniques than with effective understanding of the nature of information and its use, especially for scholarship, research, and teaching.

2. Do the content, methods, and relative balance of the several elements of professional education need revision or adjustment? For purposes of discussion, those elements (with examples of content for purposes of definition) might be identified as follows:
    - Preprofessional education
        Specified undergraduate courses
        Undergraduate concentration in pertinent fields

    - Primary professional education
        The professional role and responsibilities
        The institutional context of library operations
        Comprehensive coverage of operations and methods
        Information services for major disciplines

    - Development of specialized skills and knowledge
        Academic subjects
        Computer, telecommunications, and related text-storage technologies
        Collection management and preservation
        Financial management

    - Advanced professional education
        Organization of knowledge
        Information structure of various disciplines

    - Maintenance and enrichment of professional capabilities
        Specialized programs on management subjects
        Higher education issues
        Information policy issues

3. How can the present leaders in libraries and professional schools enlist the assistance from other disciplines that may be necessary to accomplish newly defined objectives?[4]

How these or comparable questions are answered and how the answers are translated into action will measure the maturity of the profession and will either set or remove limits on what it can contribute to teaching and learning. Viewed objectively, libraries have made exceptional progress during the past two decades and librarians have been responsible. But the fact is that the past two decades have been only a prelude to what is yet to come.

While CLR history is not, per se, the history of libraries, it is one source for such history. This record of two decades of support for librarianship is, at best, an interim report. But, given the present pace of change and the requirements implicit in the forces at work, the final report on both CLR's own efforts and a remarkable era in academic and research librarianship will be written before many more years have passed. The conclusions are, even now, being shaped.

NOTES

[1] Robert M. Hayes, ed., *Universities, Information Technology, and Academic Libraries* (Norwood, N.J.: Ablex Publishing, 1986); Basil Stuart-Stubbs, ed., *Changing Technology and Education for Librarianship and Information Science* (Greenwich, Conn.: JAI Press, 1985).

[2] Dorothy J. Anderson, "Comparative Career Profiles of Academic Librarians: Are Leaders Different?" *Journal of Academic Librarianship* 10 (January 1985):326-32.

[3] Warren J. Haas, "Information Studies, Librarianship, and Professional Leadership," *Bulletin of the Medical Library Association* 76 (January 1988):1-6.

[4] Warren J. Haas, "The Program of the Council on Library Resources," in *Les Bibliothèques: Tradition et mutation. Mélanges offerts à Jean-Pierre Clavel à l'occasion de son 65e anniversaire* (Lausanne, Switzerland: Bibliothèque cantonale et universitaire, 1987), 91-101.

2

The Influence of Computer Technology on Academic Library Buildings
A Slice of Recent History

Philip D. Leighton and David C. Weber

> We never confine ourselves to the present time. We anticipate the future as too slow in coming, as it were, to hasten its course; or we recall the past, in order to stop it as too ready to go: so imprudent, that we wander into times that are not ours, and do not think on that alone which belongs to us; and so vain, that we meditate upon those periods that have vanished, and allow the sole moment that subsists to escape without reflecting upon it.
> —Pascal, *Thoughts*

Computer-related technology is revolutionizing library operations. It is also having a strong influence on library buildings. Information technology systems and the telecommunications and power they require force building accommodations. Wiring, lighting, acoustics, environmental controls, and furniture must change to meet these systems' needs. More fundamentally, there are altered functional relationships, new library services, new social circumstances, and greatly expanded information expectations and capacities. Change seems constant and rapid.

What has been the experience and what are the current expectations for changes in academic library buildings? We begin by looking at the 1960s and the 1970s to see how computer technology first influenced library building accommodations. We then review contemporary institutional adaptations and experiences forced by rapidly expanding computer applications. And finally, we take a somewhat hazardous look five to ten years into the future, when this technology may constitute an even stronger influence on the design of new or remodeled academic library facilities.

Twenty years ago it was commonly thought that the computer would result in dramatic changes in academic library facilities. But as time passes, each change by and large hardly appears dramatic; and in most cases, with a little consideration of the factors involved, the changes seem as though they could have easily been imagined in advance. As in other historical reviews, however, the change from day to day is subtle and may hardly be perceptible, whereas cumulative adjustments over a period of even a couple of decades may actually be dramatic.

While a historian of the cultural context of science and technology might draw comparisons with the gradual changes in society brought about by the development of the radio, the electric light bulb, the phonograph, or even the elevator, each technological advance has its own unique characteristics and unanticipated consequences. Each grows within a context of economic, political, geographic, social, and organizational factors.[1] Furthermore, when a technology is in a rather early stage of development, and we do not know where to place it on a maturation curve, we later find some of the extrapolations of predicted change to be quite wild, while others may turn out to be quite close to the mark.

The fifty-year history of academic libraries using computer technology, or at least a mechanical version of it, began with data processing applications, where staff used equipment usually located in quarters outside the library. For example, in February 1936 the University of Texas Library Loan Department began processing Hollerith punched cards using IBM electric sorting machines located in the registrar's office. It is the online system and the nationwide and worldwide digital networks, however, that truly influenced building design, space allocations, and furnishings. These online systems for libraries originated during the 1960s. The last twenty years have seen rapid advancements, notably the phenomenal growth of the Online Computer Library Center (OCLC) as a descendant of the joint catalog card production effort of the medical school libraries at Yale, Columbia, and Harvard, and the unique, computer-reliant services of the Research Libraries Group (RLG) as the outgrowth of initiative by Yale, Columbia, Harvard, and the Research Libraries of the New York Public Library.

When the development of a technology is on a rapidly increasing maturation curve, we cannot then know when the rate of change slows. The pattern of historical development can be viewed accurately only when the conditions stabilize. Even with attainment of a degree of stabilization, we may not realize the full effect of a new technology for a considerable period of time (as was the case after Gutenberg's use of movable type). Will these first fifty years of the influence of computer technology on library building design span the major significant changes? Or are we only half-way toward what, in another fifty years, might be seen with hindsight as a rapid early development toward relative stability? All we can say with certainty is that the rate of progress continues to be rapid. The future influences of computer technology on library buildings will certainly continue to be very significant for another ten years, and more likely for twenty years. What have we experienced so far in this history?

THE 1960s AND 1970s

In looking back twenty years, it is evident that the first influences of computers on facilities were minimal. Buildings as a whole were not adjusted to computer technology, but rather, the technology was accommodated by retrofitting individual spaces and systems for the computer. We have selected a few college and university libraries to illustrate that phase of this history.

In the early 1960s, libraries as disparate and as distant as Harvard University and Reed College used early IBM equipment. Susan K. Martin has written that in the early 1960s, during the Widener Library shelflist conversion project, Harvard University identified and renovated space to accommodate the new systems office and nine IBM keypunch machines. Later, arrangements were made to house one of the computing center's IBM 1401 computers in the library near the systems office, and further renovation was necessary. While neither the keypunch machines nor the 1401 initially required communications lines, they needed air-conditioning and acoustic treatment. This treatment required that space separate from other library functions be assigned to the operations using this equipment. That was the first space in the library to become air-conditioned, with the circulation department following closely behind to safeguard its punched cards and batch processing equipment.[2]

The Reed College Library in 1965 started its first automation project: bookkeeping records and purchase orders printed from punched cards on the college's IBM 1130. All the work was done at the computer center and required no library space alteration. As reported by Luella Pollack, Reed's next venture was joining OCLC in 1977. OCLC use required rearrangement in the catalog department for three terminals, which entailed a compressing of functions in a large open area and the installation of an additional phone line. From the point of view of the building at Reed, there were three problems: (1) the available area forced the terminals to face a bank of windows to the east, which necessitated heavy screening; (2) there were serious problems with static, despite the static-free carpet installed after several other solutions had been tried—the problem was aggravated by prevailing winter east winds; and (3) because the OCLC line went through the college's switchboard, a campus power outage would disable the line.[3]

At Stanford University, the principal change in the late 1960s, stemming from the adoption of an acquisitions and cataloging system (the prototype for today's Research Libraries Information Network system), was the installation of a terminal cluster used by support staff. This "data control" group was located a floor above the rest of the technical processing staff because of the need for adequate staff space, group training, supervision, sound isolation, and inputting efficiency. Ironically, Stanford's first air-conditioned library spaces were not for computers but, rather, for production photocopying operations where there was a chronic problem with heat and curling paper. Air-conditioned computer rooms were always outside the library.

In most libraries, the addition of computer terminals at staff desks and the space consumed by these terminals represent perhaps the most visible changes. Except for the addition of new power circuits, carpet, and an early form of "landscape" office partitions (thought of as bank partitions, after the glass-topped panels frequently seen in banks of that era), library buildings were not significantly modified. In planning for the new technologies, staff reacted by stages to the different equipment needs by introducing appropriate tables, desks, and counters to replace earlier makeshift arrangements.

As terminals were introduced to public service desks, two arrangements became common. The first placed the terminal on a lazy susan so that after a search the staff member could turn the screen toward the reader. The other was to place the terminal at the end of a counter so that the staff member and the library patron could stand side by side to view the screen.

Noise was often a serious factor. Terminals and printers made one kind of noise; training staff and others to use the new systems generated another. In most cases, dealing with noise led to its isolation or simply acceptance. At service points, where transactions traditionally create noise, this sound was not too much of a problem. Technical processing areas, however, became nearly intolerable with the clicking and buzzing of printers. Libraries first grouped terminals (resulting in what was called the fishbowl effect), then dispersed them (resulting in the difficulty of finding an open terminal), and finally clustered them, but with a modest amount of visual and some acoustic treatment. More recently, the introduction of softer surfaces (carpeted floors, acoustic panels, and, occasionally, acoustic ceilings) and quieter printers has reduced noise problems in technical processing areas.

The association of noise with computers is in part related to human nature, for where there is no mechanical-auditory feedback (particularly with a system that is used for the input of large amounts of information), there may be a sense of feeling lost. The clicking of the keys gives useful feedback to the user of the tactile/audio system. For example, many readers have had the experience of owning an inexpensive calculator that has no tactile feedback. Without a click, the only way of knowing that something is entered (and not entered twice) is to look, which may be fine at an automated teller or possibly at a public catalog terminal. But where there is a resulting need to watch the computer screen while inputting a lengthy quote from a manuscript, the computer operator would be frustrated without tactile/audio feedback.

Fans in microcomputers also create noise, a disturbance to some even when the equipment is located in a private office. Both ink jet and laser printers can be disturbing, even though they are much quieter than the typewriters and impact printers they replace. Thus, we conclude that the nature of the technology, both in terms of its relation to humans and in terms of the physical requirements of the technology itself, will always be surrounded by some sound.

Electrical circuits represented another typical building problem because the quantity, and occasionally the quality, was frequently inadequate. Extra electrical power had to be added in all library buildings, even those designed shortly after the Second World War. To permit vertical runs from basements or ceiling spaces below, librarians arranged for coaxial cable to be pulled (sometimes using pneumatic tube runs), for abandoned central vacuum system tubes or dumbwaiter shafts to be used, or for holes to be drilled through concrete slabs. The location of columns and walls (which served as surfaces for exposed runs of conduit and surface-mounted outlet boxes) often dictated placement of equipment. "Wire management" became a necessary art.

One of the most common electrical power problems was inadequate or improper grounding. In some older buildings, the third wire required for the ground connection was not present in the AC electrical outlets or building wire plant. In others, grounding of the wires (normally through the cold water pipes or to a ground rod driven into the earth or connected to a grounding system) was not adequate. Terminals, computers, and related equipment are susceptible to many problems associated with grounding, ranging from "ground-loop" voltage, which induces errors in data transmission, to power isolation failures, which may destroy electronic components.

When the University of California at Berkeley began to use online systems, the impact of future technologies had already been anticipated, and both the acquisitions and cataloging departments were completely renovated with office landscaping, horizontal and vertical chases for wiring, and "closets" for modem pools.

Russell Shank stated that at the University of California, Los Angeles (UCLA), "We have done what a lot of libraries do—strung coaxial cables to walls at the corners of rooms and along baseboards, plugged too many microcomputers, printers, etc. into two receptacle outlets, added circuits in walls where possible for electricity, and allowed the phone company to do whatever it does to expand circuits. We have a few coaxial cables running through steam tunnels between buildings, and have drilled a few holes through thick concrete floors when it appeared necessary."[4]

As Cornell University changed to automated systems, there were problems with inadequate electrical outlets, telephone wiring, and shortages of work space and furniture as more and more microcomputers and terminals were installed. These problems continued to tax the ingenuity and patience of staff and administrators. Catherine Murray-Rust notes: "We have lived through our fair share of traumatic experiences: installing wires in foot-thick stone walls; cut cables; endless waits for the telephone company; wires shorted out when the floors are washed or waxed; once attractive offices filled with cables resembling huge piles of spaghetti; and we have survived."[5]

During the 1960s and 1970s, new library buildings were occasionally fitted with Q-decking (a flooring system with a steel pan forming the underside of a concrete slab where the steel is itself formed with lateral wire chases), cellular floors, raised floors where a mainframe might eventually be located, and knock-out plugs in anticipation of additional major cabling requirements. Cable trays above the ceiling were specified. And organized vertical chases with service closets on each floor became part of building planning, but these tended to be centralized rather than distributed, and the capacity of main ducts quickly became filled.

Lighting problems were another category of adjustment in the early accommodation to computer technology. CRTs must not have light reflected on the screen from bright sources behind, or dramatic contrast or glare from light sources in front of the reader, nor should they be under intense direct overhead light. "Landscape office" furniture dividers were brought into many locations as a way of modifying existing space to moderate those lighting problems, and local task lighting became much more prevalent. However, architects, administrators, and designers really did not adequately address lighting problems and ergonomics until the 1980s.

In the 1970s staff complained about the duration of an individual's terminal time, uncomfortable chairs, the height of tables, the emission of rays from CRTs, and noise and heat produced by CRTs. Late in the decade the lessons of ergonomics were applied to the workplace. Strongly advanced by airplane cockpit design during the 1950s, ergonomics is the engineering of space and equipment design in response to the physical and psychological requirements of humans. The computer and related devices have brought an array of relations with new tools, and many of the human factors in these relations were usually overlooked. Thus, designers studied and adjusted lighting, posture, head inclination, arm reach, and tactile and audio feedback; they also accommodated social interactive needs of those learning and applying these new systems.

In many library applications of computers, staff in technical processing units commonly had assigned times to use a shared terminal. Training quickly became more routinized and equipment more familiar, leading to a more widely spread distribution of terminals in technical services. As David McDonald (University of Michigan) has stated, some libraries seem to prefer installing one or two individual terminals in a great many locations, while others install larger banks of four, six, or even eight terminals in one place.[6] (Berkeley just completed the installation of a terminal at each cataloger's desk, which certainly suggests that soon the size of groupings will be a moot issue.) And these terminals take up ever-increasing space in all areas of the library. The cumulative effect is that older buildings are more crowded with equipment. Furthermore, work areas generally need modification in order to accommodate terminals under suitable ergonomic conditions.

Building design during the 1970s anticipated trends deriving from some of these factors. A case in point is the card catalog area in the Green Library at Stanford University, which was designed to accommodate at least eight online public access catalog (OPAC) terminals, and to provide special desk-height segments in each stand-up consultation counter for these terminals. In 1983 this configuration facilitated easy installation when the Socrates online catalog was made available to the public. (Elsewhere at Stanford, nearly all OPAC terminals are on counters.) Lighting problems, even in buildings designed in the late 1970s, remain to a large extent to be improved in the future.

THE 1980s

The past years may be characterized as accommodating older buildings and equipment to the new requirements of automation. Retrofitting was sometimes easy and was at other times difficult. What then are the current conditions?

The most significant is a recognition that building utility services must be adequate to support new requirements. Telecommunications is an issue noted by Susan K. Martin at Johns Hopkins University. "Even though the building is only 24 years old, the conduits are becoming full of the various wiring that has been installed in support of OCLC, RLIN, and the local system."[7] A number of publications deal with telecommunications, notably Heathcote.[8] Those involved with planning libraries have provided new buildings with far greater power capacity. Data communication lines are now recognized as a utility, so that they are being brought to all college and university library buildings. In a number of instances, lines are being carried to faculty studies and graduate student cubicles within these library buildings.

Even at the present time, with over twenty years of library experience with online computer systems, some of the earlier difficulties of retrofitting buildings for computer systems are still being experienced. Of problems associated with materials used in buildings, asbestos is one of the most difficult as it has prevented or made prohibitively costly the addition of cabling for computer networking in a number of older buildings. And in Stanford's Green Library, installation of lines was frustrated by the presence of metal reinforcement or metal studs in the walls, making the attachment of external cable channeling difficult.

A more extensive example is Columbia University, where Paula Kaufman has stated that office automation activities in the Butler Library began in the mid-1970s and accelerated with the introduction of microcomputers. These devices "required considerable space juggling and the installation of additional power lines" because work sites are widely dispersed on the perimeter of a very large building. While it was not difficult to make these installations, often "one found (and still finds) insufficient power on one floor and must go up or down several floors to reach the right conduits. The simultaneous introduction of RLIN terminals required more extensive efforts, and terminals were placed not always for the convenience of staff but to preserve wood paneling and floor coverings and to utilize existing power lines."

In the 1980s, Kaufman continues, "the most troublesome installation in Butler was outside the main reading room in a circulation lobby, where we finally installed 12 CLIO (OPAC) terminals. Initial plans called for the cables to be pulled to the sixth floor, dropped through the reading room's false ceiling, and run through an existing closet. This proved to be impossible: there was no way to pull the cable without damaging ornate ceiling and wood panels, and the cost of erecting scaffolding was prohibitive. The ultimate solution was to pull the cabling up through the stacks and install it under the floor, bringing it to the wall opposite the circulation desk; this meant that we had to place the machines at a site different from the original one. Campus Architect's approval to do the work, which required trenching into the marble floor base beneath the original floor covering, was required and delayed the project by several months. The original floor pieces were saved and replaced."[9]

With difficulties even in the last couple of years, Columbia was nevertheless able to overcome many aesthetic as well as technical obstacles. At Harvard, Y.T. Feng reports the same type of problems being currently faced in the Widener Library.[10] As in most academic libraries, lack of space, inflexibility of original design, and lack of an installed utility capacity make some of the problems formidable.

Regarding wiring, we are learning that the average staff work position needs at least four electrical power outlets, which will quickly be exhausted by the terminal, modem, monitor, printer, desk lamp, electric pencil sharpener, fan, calculator, clock, electric eraser, and so on. For each work station, what is desirable is a double-grounded outlet for computer or other "electronic equipment" on a dedicated circuit for such use and one or even two separate double outlets for "electrical" appliances such as lights and fans.

In older buildings, carpet tile and flat wire sometimes are an attractive way to provide access to power and signal throughout an open space. Flat wiring (e.g., ribbon cables) may have different electrical characteristics than the frequently required coaxial or twisted pair wiring which generally may not be substituted for computer signaling or networking applications. A form of phone cable and coaxial cable is available in a "flat wire" format. However, the impedance, noise immunity, and noise canceling properties of twisted and/or shielded wire are critical in many networking applications and dictate the wire types. Matching the wiring to the application becomes generally more important as the distances become larger (i.e., more than a few feet). Certainly any new facility requires many more circuits and a much broader network of distribution to provide for this need.

It is essential not to run signals together with power. Further, power circuits must be separate from those used for lighting, particularly if the lighting circuits are to be turned off each night, since certain computer systems require power to maintain their memory and thus must be left on. Indeed, a microcomputer file can be lost if lights are blinked to warn readers before the building closes.

In addition to power, computers need links to networks accommodated via twisted copper wire pairs, fiber optic cable and/or coaxial cable. At this time the library can expect both twisted pairs and coaxial to be distributed to each computer station. Fiber optics will certainly enter the library building, but currently they terminate in a "node" located in a closet or phone room. The need for a wiring closet of substantial size is increasing, and phone rooms in older buildings will become increasingly difficult to deal with in the future because of a typical lack of space for both wire/cable connections and for equipment. These distribution closets must not only be larger but must have environmental controls and power for active electronic components. Further, the vertical chases and service closets are becoming more widely distributed in large buildings to ease the future connections to computer-linked systems.

Networking in buildings has become as necessary a service utility as the telephone. To provide effectively for this new utility, the institution needs to adopt a building signal wiring standard that provides a harness, that is, telephone, computer, terminal, and video services preferably at a single wall outlet. In the past, networks have been installed in buildings on a piecemeal basis and tailored to the needs of the client, often after the building has been constructed. Because of this piecemeal approach, managers have on occasion made mistakes and caused inefficiencies in installing communications facilities in buildings. Links to other buildings on campus and off campus are now required.

Designers can reduce or eliminate problems by integrating the planning and installation of these communication services. Experience at Stanford indicates that savings of as much as 40 percent of the wiring cost are possible when compared with separate telephone and local area network (LAN) installation. There are additional benefits, too. The delivery of multiple services to a single wall plate is not practical unless the design and installation are done as one project. Documentation and maintenance of signal distribution systems is simplified. And integrity of the installation is higher because the probability of damage to one system in the course of installing another is reduced. Therefore, at Stanford University, the telephone and network wiring for new buildings, like the other utility facilities that are part of the building, is now combined under a single standard and included as part of the capital cost for each building project.

There have been some difficulties in combining computer and other electronic technologies with certain book detection systems. In some cases, the computer terminal itself will set off the detection system or the detection system will interfere with the operation of the computer. Reducing the sensitivity of the detection system, moving the terminal away from the detection screen, or adding special shielding to the computer terminals has solved this problem in most cases.

A second concern with security systems deals with the floppy disk. Some libraries (Washington State University is an example) have made arrangements to pass the disks around security detection screens even though the vendors of the security system claim this is not necessary. It is very clear, however, that any magnetic storage device must be kept well away from the security system device that alters the magnetism of a strip of material in the book. This procedure should not present an overwhelming problem until there is a substantial number of books with floppy disks in them. In this case, there must be special handling of materials associated with magnetic memory devices in the check-out process.

Heat became less of a concern as vacuum tubes gradually gave way to transistors and solid state circuitry, yet equipment grouped together can still create a serious problem. File servers on a local network and/or minicomputers produce a considerable amount of heat as well. Reed College Library indicated that one reason for choosing a particular automated system was the fact that it did not need a climate-controlled environment. Yet, with Reed's microcomputers in a large catalog department space, the combination of lights, people, and computer equipment generates enough heat to create unpleasant working conditions in the summer.

Online catalogs with printers are found in growing numbers of libraries (including Stanford's), and laser jet and ink jet printers make it possible to provide that service without noise difficulties in most public parts of the library. In the current building design for Mills College, the library is planning all online catalog consultation stations to be at stand-up counter height in order to discourage users from spending unnecessarily long periods of time at the terminal. Typically, libraries have at least two-thirds of the OPAC terminals on stand-up counters, with a very few at sit-down height; the latter can be sought out by an individual with a long and complex task or by a patron in a wheelchair. OPAC terminals are also placed on stack floors and in periodical reading rooms. Sunken circulation counter areas for automated equipment are reasonably common. Reference desks can now obviate the need for a lazy susan by merely plugging in a patron monitor screen. Thus, the staff can search at the control terminal while conversing with a patron who watches the slave monitor faced in the opposite direction across the desk or counter.

At Pennsylvania State University Library, as described by Bruce D. Bonta, "One of the most critical issues ... is the physical placement and arrangement of new CD-ROM equipment. Since we believe that these indexes and services should be placed in close conjunction with the print volumes that they complement, we are having a lot of problems accommodating them physically. The reference room provides a spacious, effective area for the use of about 40,000 reference works, hundreds of indexes and abstracts, many on large index tables, plus special areas such as the reference microfiche area. Opened in 1972, the room does not allow for the power needs, data transmission, or other communication possibilities that the CD-ROM technology requires. Most of the room has a coffered concrete ceiling, the floor is a 16" thick concrete slab that defies drilling, and the only power is available at the concrete support columns 22' apart. The present placement of the (library automated system) terminals, microfiche readers, CD-ROM stations, plus other electronic equipment used by patrons had taken nearly all of the available column locations. Placing a CD-ROM product that includes a data transmission feature from a remote computer, such as the WilsonDisc services, will be difficult for us without a lot of construction costs."[11]

For interlibrary lending services, the computer offers an alternative means of transmitting information. Libraries commonly transmit photocopies by mail. A few libraries have experimented with telefacsimile machines to transmit pages, but the staff time, telephone expense and length of transmission time have ordinarily made it difficult to justify this technology. The computer, with the ability to transmit large amounts of information digitally, offers a communication technology that will be advantageous to interlibrary loan.

While use of computer software requires training, the nature of the training will vary depending on the nature of the program as well as the people involved. There is a need within the academic institution for spaces where organized instruction can be provided. Such space can be thought of as being part of the library function in ways similar to bibliographic instruction. Both computer instruction and bibliographic instruction are necessary for access to and manipulation of information. For faculty, a separate room is sometimes provided for self-education, arranged in such a way that one can seek help and yet not feel embarrassment. However, Drexel University, which originally had a separate faculty room, found that separation was soon not needed. Students accept training as part of a course, but if it is not required, they also usually prefer a self-help environment.

In many libraries, typing rooms or small classrooms have been converted to microcomputer labs or to online classrooms for bibliographic and computer instruction, and for computer-assisted general course work. Cornell transformed two small public reading rooms into such facilities, and, while the renovations were modest, the educational effect of these facilities was substantial because of their heavy and successful use. At Cornell, Michigan, Stanford, and elsewhere, libraries have student microcomputer labs and public access terminals with more than 100 pieces of equipment and with some additional number available for faculty. Yet, at Williams College, Phyllis Cutler indicates that the library refused to give up reader space for personal computers (PCs), believing that noise would be a problem and that reading spaces should not be reduced in number; it did put thirty PCs in enclosed conference spaces.[12] Librarians must help determine whether provision of PCs should take up more space in academic libraries, or whether separate facilities apart from the library should be the norm. Increasingly, terminals are located in residence halls, with a student guru to provide local help, to decentralize general access to computer technology.

The social and privacy aspects of using computer technology are unresolved. Observation suggests that some students and many faculty are actually quite shy when they first face computer technology. They prefer to have semiprivate quarters in which to learn and perhaps to stumble while using the system. Steven Pandolfo of Mills College believes that those performing searches appreciate real privacy as well as quiet.[13] At UCLA, however, there are no places where there are private facilities and, Russell Shank reports, "if the faculty are troubled in any way, they don't let us know."[14] At some institutions such as Reed College, the privacy aspect has been met by facilitating access to the catalog via modem from any faculty office on campus and from home.

People are social creatures, and there is a clear social aspect of many computer processes. Both library staff and library users need help and wish to discuss their experiences. Some people need little privacy and tolerate sound and commotion, while others feel quite the opposite, and libraries must accommodate this diversity. People interact more when using computers than when using most earlier technologies dealing with information. This socializing is due to a number of factors, including the reaction when the wrong key is hit, the waiting for something to happen (a fine time to say hello to your neighbor), the general confusion and lack of certainty (and thus the desire to ask "what now") as new computer users learn the systems, and so on. When computer-related activities are being introduced, conversation and teaching should be facilitated at some workstations since the need for help may occur at unpredictable times.[15]

If the first ten or fifteen years of online computer systems in academic libraries was a period of modest adjustment, recently there has been greater change (notably stemming from the OPAC and microcomputer clusters) and much better understanding of how people and automated systems interact. Spaces have been more satisfactorily adjusted to accommodate the human needs. New buildings and the renovation of older buildings have led to less awkwardness in using new technology. Further, as Harold W. Billings reports of the University of Texas, "the ubiquitousness of the micro computer/terminal throughout the library is, of course, obvious, but the hegira of the library terminal to non-library locations (and the lack of a need to provide large areas for a central library computer, as we believed we would require ten years ago) is quite striking."[16] And what of the future?

THE 1990s

We project that the next five to ten years will see the equipment supporting computer technology becoming so common in staff offices and public areas that people will view computer access and transmission devices as an unsurprising advance over the combined services of the typewriter, the telephone, the photocopy machine, and others in the extended family of information systems. Among changes coming about from multitasking and distributed processing and standards for linking technologies is the capacity through a single workstation to connect with a variety of databases and information systems. A person will be able to move easily back and forth, without having to deal with a different piece of hardware and a different query structure for each system.[17]

Carrying that a step further, we can expect that the workstations and information systems they connect with will be developed in a variety of models, some of which have great power and system elegance. Designers will create furniture to house the microcomputers that will be much more appropriate and flexible.[18] The personal workstation will have a keyboard integrated into a comfortable chair, with a printer attached and facsimile transmission capabilities included. Architects will design improved space and environmental conditions for workstations.[19]

There will continue to be rationale for traditional access to library materials (walking to the shelf and fetching a book, for example) and using computers for bibliographic control. Only to a very limited degree will computers be used for full text until late in the next decade. However, electronic publishing of heavily used materials, such as journals and major reference works, will come more rapidly than for the general collections, which tend to be much less heavily used than computer technology would economically support at this time.

Concerning seating for readers, the traditional functions of the library will continue and will be supplemented by the computer to a large extent. Significant changes will result in the configuration and operation of reading areas, the reference area, service points in general, and interlibrary loan, as well as spaces outside of the library by way of which one will be able to access information managed by or through the library.

And where and how will students use the PCs in class written work? With the ability to transmit digitized information comes the ability to manage that information and use it directly in the process of creating a paper for a classroom assignment. Initially the writing process may be heaviest within the library, simply because that is where access to the necessary networks and databases will be provided and facilitated, both in terms of the physical equipment and connections and staff assistance. As these devices will continue to be used along with traditional materials, the library as a site for this function makes a lot of sense for some students, though not for many others.

One postulate is that because of access to computers in the dormitory, the student culture will change to the degree necessary to support study in dormitories (a practice that at most times—exam time being an exception—has been virtually impossible because of student activities), and that the need for study space in libraries will diminish in the future, to be replaced with a need to provide facilities to supplement the student's PC capacity. These facilities may consist of publishing centers, training centers, a reserve desk for assigned software packages, and computer clusters. These clusters may have configurations supportive of networking, language practice, use of extensive computational equipment, or other activities seldom available on individual computers. Many of these functions are already visible in libraries.

We believe, on the other hand, that students will continue to find ways to disrupt serious study in the dormitory and that other sites—particularly the library—will continue to be in heavy demand for serious reading in quiet spaces and for the use of computers in support of study, course work, and research.

The large reference collection of thousands of volumes may in the future be reduced as more services are available and used online. Already in the 1980s, indexing and abstracting services are much less used in print form, and optical disk stations will take some of that space. We believe that the use of the reference room will increase demand upon space, rather than diminish it, as the need for database searching, teaching, and other computer-based work will not be easily offset by any possible reduction in the collections. And, we are quite sure that the traditional book as we know it will remain, even in the reference room.

In relation to further design adjustments in library space planning, there are many questions. Will some staff work at home? Can the location of the catalog department be on a different floor from the main public catalog, or even in a different building? Will the technical processing functions be decentralized to a greater degree than at present? Can the interlibrary loan service be remote from the reference collection and the public catalog? Will library quarters include online classrooms? Will seating in libraries as a percentage of enrollment decrease slightly as students use a local area network to access information systems from distributed microcomputer laboratories and dormitory rooms? Will libraries need to accommodate portable computer devices brought in by library users for notetaking purposes? Will public workstations in libraries need to be arranged to accommodate considerable diversity in the physical and environmental preferences of readers? Will security of institutional equipment continue to be a significant concern?

The answer to each of these questions is yes, to some degree. Technological advancement, ease and simplicity of use, and financial considerations will strongly influence the rate of progress and the exact shape of the development.[20]

Let us expand this point by commenting on one aspect: portability. Currently, computers are not easily portable, and it is unlikely that staff will soon wish to read a computer screen while taking the bus to work, despite lap models with thin liquid crystal display (LCD) screens. Computers occasionally carried by library users will be small, battery-powered and quiet; they will, despite some sound, be used even in an open reading room to record notes, quotations, or citations. Although workstations can be on wheels for greater portability, dependable links to communications lines are necessary and the faster systems of communications will be on networks that are considerably more sophisticated than the present common phone line. Each phone jack may also have a computer jack, and the computer can be taken from station to station when those jacks remain constantly "hot" (a practice currently discouraged by the pricing of telephone service through the Gandalf data switch but commonly free on campus network connections).

Thus, it seems reasonable to predict that, over the next decade, the computer will not be an instrument that is carried around more than was the portable typewriter in the 1950s. The real workhorse for readers as well as staff will remain a unit that is not portable. In using ubiquitous stationary equipment, people will carry information in the form of floppy disks, optical disks, at least for the near term. Or, they will call up their data from a centralized file server to the workstation at which they are currently seated, and it will be sent over a high-speed communication network.

The general lack of portability also suggests that the book and notebook will be with us for a long time. Even if cost is not an acceptable argument for the desirability of traditional over high-tech formats, there are very practical reasons supporting the traditional technology—the book. It is a universally familiar format, compact, portable, attractive, often indexed, and readily accessed to any chapter or page. It facilitates, much more easily than does a database, the scanning or creative serendipity of reading a volume. And all one needs is adequate light for reading anywhere in the world. Meanwhile, with a growing level of computer literacy and use, the computer will extend the capacity to know of the existence of books and other units of information, to find these items, to copy and transmit them, and to expand greatly the manipulative handling of information. Libraries therefore will not shrink, but rather grow and add an entirely new information management technology, expanding the library function and requiring a host of building adjustments.

At present, the concept of "smart buildings" is emerging. Smart buildings, sometimes called "intelligent buildings," have sophisticated technology, including computer-controlled card entrance and egress, computer-controlled environmental management, sophisticated data reception both on dedicated lines and by microwave transmitters, and electric power and dataline outlets in every room in a number of locations with enough capacity for double or triple the current maximum requirement of the typical high-tech library office.[21] In the coming decade this electronically advanced design may be a strong influence over library building planning, especially planning to accommodate computer technology.

In smart library buildings, multiple vertical shafts with horizontal distribution ducts will be common for adapting to future change. Designers will provide spaces, probably on each floor and in many cases several on each floor, for the equipment required to change from fiber optic transmission to coaxial or wire transmissions. These wiring closets of the future will be air-conditioned, for they may house network servers (computers, storage devices, etc.), and electronics. The library must house line filters or surge suppressors, often centrally in the wire closets. Lighting, including light levels, should be designed for computers and controlled by computers. Computers will monitor and control energy use. And the budget and the competition for space will more likely limit the capacity to install computer-supported systems than will power and signal (which seldom were truly limiting factors in the past). Technological skill will continue to make the computer smaller, cooler, easier to read, easier to use, more ergonomic, and so on. All of which suggests that the technology itself is changing more dramatically than the facilities that use and house the technology.

Operational changes in the library will come about as the technology requires or permits. Librarians will use card catalogs only for specialized uses such as miniaturized illustrations of prints mounted on cards. Library systems staff offices will remain in the building and grow in size as staff increases. There will be common use of machine-readable user cards, card-key controlled access to restricted areas, and printers distributed as photocopiers have been; and it can be hoped that digitized full-text transmission directly from bound materials will be economically provided. Despite use of battery-powered computers, outlets will need to be widely available for terminals that library users carry. Desks, counters and tables, and chairs, will take on new configurations in accommodating to the human activities of an advanced technological era.

Thus, in conclusion, it is evident that libraries are only beginning to move into the sophisticated age of information technology. The next ten years will see many further subtle changes in the work place, some few significant functional relocations in new library buildings, and a more human-sensitive environment for using microcomputers and terminals. These developments will not come without cost. Perhaps the biggest unknown is the influence on this rate of development that derives from the national economy, as suggested below.

There can be little question that computer systems as they benefit library management and services are still developing at a rapid rate. They have not reached maturity by any means. And the rate at which laboratory developments can be turned into practical operating systems will also be conditioned by the profit possibilities of systems that are of interest to libraries. Unless the particular system is broadly supported in the general commercial sense, it probably will be too expensive for libraries to support.

It is therefore anyone's guess whether the world of higher education and scholarship can have funds available to enable libraries on college and university campuses to use the technology as fast as it is developed. If, in fact, there is a demonstrable benefit to the educational process, either in terms of the quality or rapidity of learning, or if the economics of higher education can be significantly improved, then one can suppose that funds would be available to advance information systems rapidly. On the other hand, if those benefits do not materialize or if the general economy is weak, it may be a long time before the more sophisticated advances in the laboratory are available in academic libraries.

In the meantime, there is every reason for enthusiasm about the advances that have been and are being made. The progress of the past three decades constitutes an exciting slice of library history.

Many items must be considered when planning a new building. Lighting issues involve the elimination of glare and the provision of power for computers separate from lighting circuits. Acoustical issues include the social aspects of computer use as well as the mechanical noise produced by the equipment, and the need to control or minimize the influence of noise on the more traditional use of libraries. Planners must consider the interaction of computer terminals with other systems, such as book security systems and information transmission systems, because they may be affected by electronic noise and power lines. General issues include space, portability, ergonomics, signal distribution, control of static electricity, power access, and security. The concept of a "smart" building may influence future building planning.

What is the effect of automated systems on other operations such as card catalogs, technical processing, access to remote databases by scholars, the function of the reference desk, and the process of teaching scholars how to use the computer effectively in support of research? The ability to transmit information and to access information from computer terminals will affect the way scholars use a library. And finally, but perhaps most importantly, what ramifications will emerge from the fact that the traditional book, book stacks, and reading areas will continue to be required as far into the future as we can see.

NOTES

[1] Professor Thomas Parke Hughes, writing in *Networks of Power: Electrification in Western Society, 1880-1930* (Baltimore: Johns Hopkins University Press, 1983), describes five phases in the evolution of complex technological systems. First comes the invention and development. Second is the process of technology transfer from one application and society to others. Third is system growth through resolution of system irregularities, critical problems, and component lags. Fourth comes substantial momentum providing an inertia of directed motion, often with rate accelerating and influenced by government agencies, professional societies, educational institutions, and strong business concerns. And the fifth phase finds financiers and technologists expert in very large systems coping with problems of maturing growth (see pp. 14-17).

[2] Susan K. Martin, Director, Milton S. Eisenhower Library, The Johns Hopkins University, letter to author, September 1987.

[3] Luella R. Pollack, Director, E.V. Hauser Memorial Library, letter to author, September 2, 1987.

[4] Russell Shank, University Librarian, University of California at Los Angeles, letter to author, September 8, 1987.

[5] Catherine Murray-Rust, Assistant to the University Librarian, Cornell University Libraries, letter to author, September 17, 1987.

[6] David R. McDonald, Systems Librarian, University Library, University of Michigan, Ann Arbor, letter to author, August 11, 1987.

[7] Susan K. Martin, letter to author, September 1987.

[8] Denis Heathcote and Peter Stubley, "Building Services and Environmental Needs of Information Technology in Academic Libraries," *Program* 1, no. 1

(January 1986): 26-38. See also Peter Stubley, "Equipment and Furniture to Meet the Requirements of the New Technology," paper read at the Eighth International Federation of Library Associations and Institutions Seminar on Library Buildings, Aberystwyth, Wales, August 1987.

[9] Paula T. Kaufman, Acting Vice President for Information Services and University Librarian, Columbia University, letter to author, August 26, 1987.

[10] Yen-Tsai Feng, Librarian of Harvard College, telephone conversation with author, September 1987.

[11] Bruce D. Bonta, "CD-Rom in the Social Science Reference Room," paper presented at International Federation of Library Associations and Institutions, Brighton, England, August 1987.

[12] Phyllis L. Cutler, Director, Williams College, telephone conversation with author, September 1987.

[13] Steven P. Pandolfo, College Librarian, Mills College, letter to author, August 21, 1987.

[14] Russell Shank, letter to author, September 8, 1987.

[15] The social influence has also been dealt with in a paper at the ACRL Seattle conference: David C. Weber, "The Impact of Computer Technology on Academic Library Buildings," in *Academic Libraries: Myths and Realities*, ed. Suzanne C. Dodson and Gary L. Menges (Chicago: Association of College and Research Libraries, 1984), 202.

[16] Harold W. Billings, Director, University of Texas Libraries, Austin, letter to author, November 18, 1987.

[17] Carrol D. Lunau, "The Use of Electronic Mail and Interlibrary Loan Automation in Canada," paper presented at International Federation of Library Associations and Institutions, Brighton, England, August 1987.

[18] See especially Margaret Beckman, "Library Equipment in a Changing Library Environment," paper read at International Federation of Library Associations and Institutions, Brighton, England, August 1987.

[19] Heathcote and Stubley, "Building Services"; Stubley, "Equipment and Furniture."

[20]Some general guidance can be found in Elaine and Aaron Cohen, *Automation, Space Management and Productivity* (N.Y.: Bowker, 1981) and in Roscoe Rouse, Jr., "Planning Tomorrow's Library Building Today," paper presented at the Oklahoma Network of Continuing Higher Education Leadership Seminar, Norman, October 3, 1986.

[21]One treatment is by Dean Schwenke, *Smart Buildings and Technology—Enhanced Real Estate*, Washington, D.C.: The Urban Land Institute, 1985.

3

Retrieval of Information from Computerized Book Texts

Frederick G. Kilgour

This paper describes the use of tables of contents and back-of-the-book indexes in electronic form produced by traditional techniques of human full-text analysis. Such indexes greatly increase access to library-like information in terms both of immediacy and availability and are superior to computerized full-text searching because of their topical and cross-reference entries. First, I will present a brief description of the overall design of EIDOS (Electronic Information Delivery Online System). Following are an account of the EIDOS databases, a progress report on the research for and the development of EIDOS, a discussion of users' use of books, and the benefits of EIDOS.

EIDOS, in development at the Online Computer Library Center (OCLC), is an interactive, online method for retrieving information from written books that are in digital form. Figure 3.1 depicts the system. The information seeker at a microcomputer retrieves either the book's table of contents or its index, selects an entry, requests the page of the text by location number, and receives the page on the monitor. An example of this procedure is obtaining information on the cost of online cataloging in a public library from Donald Sager's *Public Library Administrators' Planning Guide to Automation*.[1] The seeker of this information (1) retrieves the catalog entry for Sager's work by author or title, by author and title, or by subject; (2) obtains the index and locates "Cost estimating for online cataloging. 92-94" and requests "p 92"; and (3) when page 92 appears on the screen, finds a listing of "Cost elements associated with online cataloging" and related information.

Entries for topics and concepts not named in the text, which are abundant in traditional book indexes, make human-produced indexes superior to machine-produced indexes and to full-text searches. Recently two mature scholars possessing three thoughtful decades of experience in information processing and investigation discussed this aspect of retrieval. J.C. Gardin stated, "After 30 years of research conducted on a world scale, we still do not know how to communicate to our computers, old or young, the intelligence which they would need to demonstrate, *unaided*, translation and indexing abilities approaching those of their human counterparts. We therefore continue to rely on translators for translation, and on librarians, indexers or the authors themselves for

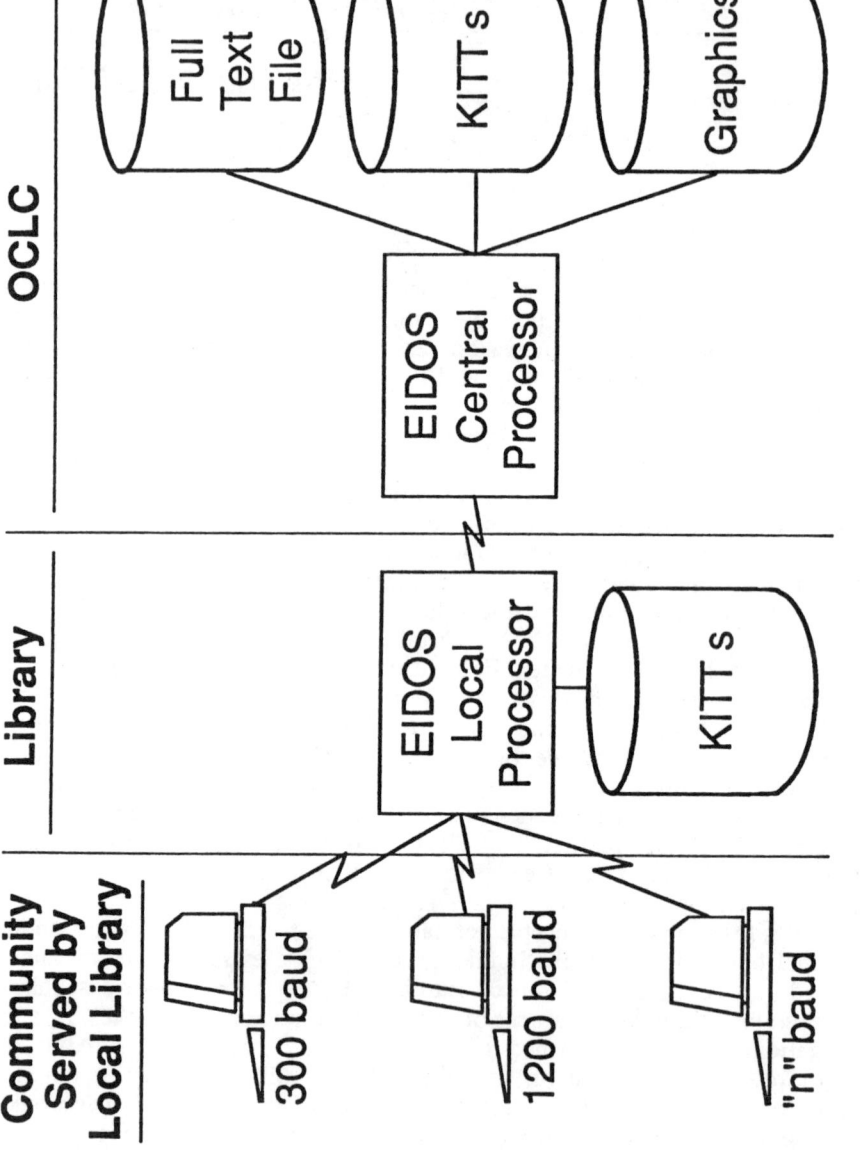

Fig. 3.1. EIDOS system architecture.

classification and indexing. Needless to say, we are nevertheless in favour of continuing research on those processes, until we succeed in developing intelligent systems up to human standards."[2] D.R. Swanson reasoned "that consistently effective fully automatic indexing and retrieval is not possible" and added, "that is not to deny that machines are unsurpassed as an aid to information retrieval, and that continued research to improve such capacity is warranted."[3]

SYSTEM PURPOSE AND DESIGN

The purpose of EIDOS is to promote the welfare and effectiveness of people by making information increasingly available. EIDOS has three goals, the first of which is to provide immediate availability of information in electronic form to any user at any time. It will do this by operating twenty-four hours and by enabling information seekers to access its databases from microcomputers in homes, offices, schools and universities, and libraries. At the present time, only fifty-nine of every hundred users entering libraries are successful in obtaining books they seek. EIDOS will increase this success rate by 47 percent, primarily because an electronic book is always available.[4]

Initially, EIDOS will operate with only books in its databases, but long-range plans call for adding other library materials such as journal articles and maps, as well as materials now generally unavailable—for example, informational radio and television programs. Provision of traditional as well as nontraditional information sources will enable EIDOS to achieve its second goal, which is to increase the scope and quantity of available information.

Economies of scale will enable EIDOS to achieve its third goal, an improved user-satisfaction/producer-cost ratio.

It is anticipated that the vast majority of accesses will be via microcomputers from home, workplace, and academe. Experience of at least one other online system is that over half of such micros function as dumb terminals in online searches. EIDOS, however, will also provide displays for micros possessing graphics and windowing capabilities. The design includes searches to retrieve a single item swiftly and accurately, as well as multiple items containing specific subject information. Derived truncated search keys will recall a single author, title, or subject heading swiftly and accurately, while keyword and implied Boolean searching will retrieve subject groupings. Full Boolean searching will not be available, for as one experienced author has put it, "if you use Boolean operators, heaven help you, it is also the ultimate in trivial pursuits."[5]

Equipment at the local site consists of a processor, its database of KITTs (variable-length records containing *K*eys to access, *I*ndex, *T*able of contents, and the *T*itle information for books in the central database), and a supplemental database of graphics from each book represented by a KITT in the local database. Upon receipt of a search request, the local processor conducts the search in its database of KITTs. Once a seeker has identified a page number in either the table of contents or index displayed on the monitor and has requested the page by location number, the local processor forwards the request to the central site.

Equipment at the central site consists of the central processor with its large database of book texts, the database containing indexes to the database of texts, and supplementary KITT and graphics databases. When the central processor receives a request for a page, it retrieves that page as well as the preceding page and the following page and transmits the three pages to the local processor, which formats and displays the requested page on the seeker's monitor. Should the seeker then request either the preceding or following page, the local processor displays it immediately and requests the central site to transmit the page sequentially beyond the page displayed. If the seeker originally requested page 35, the central site would transmit 35 as well as 34 and 36 to be available for immediate display. Then if the seeker requested 34, the local site would immediately display 34 and request 33, which would be overwritten on 36.

DATABASE CONSTRUCTION

There are four possible sources of machine-readable books: (1) printed books scanned by optical character recognition to convert texts, and by bit mapping to convert graphics; (2) keyboarded texts and scanned graphics; (3) photocomposition text tapes that may or may not contain final page-proof corrections and graphics; and (4) text tapes containing texts with final corrections and Standard Generalized Markup Language (SGML) but with graphics not included. EIDOS has been using photocomposition tapes supplied by publishers; one publisher has also supplied EIDOS with SGML tapes.

Publishers send EIDOS weekly internal news sheets that track the progress of books through the publishing process from manuscript to printing, from which EIDOS requests selected titles for inclusion in the system. Upon receipt, each book is examined to see if it possesses both a table of contents and an index; lack of either causes rejection. If it contains both, its index is then evaluated against the criteria in table 3.1. Each of the first two criteria is of the utmost importance; failure to meet only one of them results in rejection. Failure to meet only one of the next three criteria could cause rejection. Although each of the last four is important, failure to meet only one might not cause rejection.

Table 3.1.
Criteria for evaluating indexes

1. Cross-references must be present.

2. Topics and concepts in the text must be represented by appropriate terms.

3. Significant items in the text must appear in the index.

4. Entries must be in correct order.

5. Page location numbers in the index must be correct.

6. Chapter headings, subheadings, and captions should be indexed.

7. Density of entries should be at least two to a page of text.

8. The index should be comprehensive.

9. There must be consistency among entries.

When a book has been approved, EIDOS requests from the publisher a photocomposition tape and two printed copies to be guillotined for scanning graphics.

EIDOS staff members examine and analyze the tape and prepare a computer program to remove most of the photocomposition language from the tape. Some commands are translated to SGML to be used in subsequent formatting for display, and some that should have been removed but were not are erased manually. Once this process is complete, the machine-readable tape is EIDOS-usable. An SGML tape from the one publisher that can supply this format requires less than half the time to process as does a photocomposition tape.

Next, a staff member makes the EIDOS-usable tape human-usable by editing. This process involves manually adding page numbers, inserting the instruction for obtaining a graphic in the position that the graphic occupies in the printed text, and restoring hyphens in compound words deleted when they occurred at the end of a printed line. The book is then cataloged on the OCLC system, and the catalog version of the MARC record is attached to the front of the machine-readable text, which is then loaded into the central database.

Next, a set of programs constructs the KITT by writing out the MARC record, table of contents, and index. The system then constructs from the data in the MARC record the derived truncated search keys to locate the KITT by author, author/title, title, and subject heading, as well as by keyword keys. When the KITT is complete it is loaded into the central KITT database. On demand, copies will be made and downloaded to local processors.

While all this activity is going on, the printed book is being guillotined and fed into a scanner to digitize its graphics. These bit-mapped graphics are related to the machine-readable book by pointers to their precise location in the text. Next, the graphics are loaded into the central graphics database ready to accompany its respective KITT downline to a local processor.

RESEARCH AND DEVELOPMENT

Two recent studies have revealed that EIDOS will dramatically improve availability of information in books. The first found that only 59 percent of people entering a library to obtain a book actually are successful in doing so. Eleven fail because the book has been lent, eight because of inadequate (and unimprovable) library procedures, and five because, for various reasons, they did not find the book on the shelf.[6] The second study found that an additional five failed because they erred in searching the catalog or the catalog was defective.[7] EIDOS will eliminate these twenty-eight failures, thereby making it possible for eighty-seven of every 100 users to obtain desired information rapidly and accurately.

OCLC has sponsored four studies to investigate the manner in which people use books, because only one (inadequate) study (1949) had been carried out in this area of the unknown. Gordon A. and Patricia L. Sabine published an investigation entitled "How People Use Books and Journals."[8] M.Y. Gates published *A Study of How Books Are Used*[9] reporting research in the United Kingdom, and Chandra Prabha with her colleagues at OCLC carried out two investigations, one at the Public Library of Columbus and Franklin County (Ohio),[10] and the other at the main library of The Ohio State University, also in Columbus.[11]

Tables 3.2 through 3.4 are based on findings in these four studies. Table 3.2 reports the proportion of a book used. It has been of considerable importance to EIDOS to learn that three of the four studies in table 3.2 found that, of those consulting books, between 41.1 and 48.1 percent used only 25 percent of the book or less. Table 3.3 reveals equally important findings: (1) of persons seeking information in books, between 43.8 and 75.7 percent sought specific

Table 3.2.
Proportion of book used by percent

Study	25% or less	50% or less
Gates	41.1	— —
Prabha (CPL)	23.0	29.7
Prabha (OSU)	42.7	62.4
Sabine	48.1†	73.9

†15 percent or less

Table 3.3.
Percent of book users seeking information

Study	Specific information	Specific plus general information	Success in finding specific plus general information
Gates	65.7		
Prabha (CPL)	43.8	88.2	84.4
Prabha (OSU)	75.7	97.3	91.7

information, and (2) 88.2 and 97.3 percent of persons seeking general as well as specific information were successful 84.4 and 91.7 percent of the time.

Table 3.4 contains a surprise in that both public library and university library users employed the back-of-the-book index less often than the table of contents or scanning of the entire book. However, in the university, exclusive users of tables of contents plus indexes outnumber those using scanning exclusively, and the combination of those using tables of contents and indexes together with another method or methods is more than twice those using scanning together with other methods. Although public library users employ exclusive scanning twice as often as combined exclusive use of tables of contents and indexes, the combination of those using tables of contents or indexes plus some other method equals those who scan and use another method.

Table 3.4.

Three major methods for locating information in books

Study	Exclusive use	Exclusive use plus other methods
Prabha (CPL)		
Scanning entire book	40.1	58.7
Consulting table of contents	10.5	35.8
Consulting index	13.2	27.2
Prabha (OSU)		
Scanning entire book	21.1	44.2
Consulting table of contents	17.5	61.2
Consulting index	6.9	40.3

Development of EIDOS began in the autumn of 1983, and a prototype was first demonstrated in London in December 1984,[12] and, after improvement, in Paris in June 1985. Since summer 1985, EIDOS has concentrated on developing an operational system. The present schedule calls for the pilot model of the system, depicted in figure 3.1 (see page 32), to be working by summer 1989.

BENEFITS OF MATURE EIDOS

Libraries in the United States have been experiencing decreasing financial support in the last decade and a half in that their expenses have been rising more rapidly than the funds allocated to them. With their users frustrated two-fifths of the time because of inability to obtain desired materials, there is no general clamor to spend more money on libraries. EIDOS will reduce the frustration from two-fifths to one-eighth, which should certainly turn the present user apathy into enthusiastic support.

EIDOS will also reduce library expenditures. For books, a mature EIDOS operation will eliminate, not just reduce but eliminate, cataloging costs, physical processing, shelving, lending, and reshelving, and will make it unnecessary to construct new buildings to house books. Library operating costs might be reduced by as much as 25 percent. Although such costs are not readily available in the literature, cost of cataloging alone appears to be nearly a fifth of total library costs. At Washington University's Olin Library System, salaries in Cataloging and Classification Services are 17 percent of total library salaries.[13] The positions in cataloging at The Ohio State University Libraries constitute 20.6 percent of the total regular staff.[14] Salary and nonsalary operating costs plus direct and overhead costs for cataloging of monographs at the University of Wellington in Canada are 34 percent of the total of such costs for collections development, acquisition and cataloging of monographs and serials, information services, circulation of library materials, and interlibrary loans.[15]

For publishers, EIDOS will both increase revenues and decrease costs. Sale of KITTs to libraries, which will surely stimulate overall sales (including print copies), will increase revenues. Publishers' expenses will decrease with respect to their revenue from EIDOS sales of KITTs, for they will not incur the expense of printing, binding, warehousing, retrieving, packaging, and invoicing.

Information seekers will benefit most from a mature EIDOS even if it were to contain only books, for availability of information within books will increase by half. These searchers will also obtain desired information immediately on microcomputers at their home or workplace. And finally, they will not pay for the information they receive because EIDOS design incorporates the library practice of not charging users.

NOTES

[1]Donald J. Sager, *Public Library Administrator's Planning Guide to Automation* (Dublin, Ohio: Online Computer Library Center, 1983).

[2]Jean-Claude Gardin, *Expert Systems and Scholarly Publications* (London: The British Library, 1987).

[3] Don R. Swanson, "Historical Note: Information Retrieval and the Future of an Illusion," *Journal of the American Society for Information Science* 39 (March 1988):92-98.

[4] Frederick G. Kilgour, "EIDOS: 100 Percent Shelf Availability and Reduced Failure in Access to Books," in press, and Frederick G. Kilgour, "Reduction in Catalog Search Failures by the Electronic Information Delivery Online System (EIDOS)," in press.

[5] Bette S. Brunelle, "The Production of a Full-Text Database," in *Proceedings of the Sixth National Online Meeting, New York, April 30-May 2, 1985*, comps. Martha E. Williams and Thomas H. Hogan (Medford, N.J.: Learned Information, 1985), 72.

[6] Kilgour, "EIDOS: 100 Percent Shelf Availability."

[7] Kilgour, "Reduction in Catalog Search Failures."

[8] Gordon A. Sabine, and Patricia L. Sabine, "How People Use Books and Journals," *Library Quarterly* 56 (October 1986):399-408.

[9] M. Y. Gates, *A Study of How Books Are Used* (Dublin, Ohio: Online Computer Library Center, 1987).

[10] Chandra Prabha, John Bunge, and Duane Rice, *How Public Library Patrons Use Nonfiction Books* (Dublin, Ohio: Online Computer Library Center, 1987).

[11] Chandra Prabha, Duane Rice, and Dave Cameron, *Nonfiction Book Use by Academic Library Patrons*, in press.

[12] Frederick G. Kilgour, Betsy N. Kiser, and Georgia Brown, "An Electronic Information Delivery Online System," in *Proceedings of the 8th International Online Meeting, London, 4-6 December 1984* (Oxford: Learned Information, 1984), 171-77.

[13] Otha Overholt, Director of Technical Services and Library Systems, personal communication to author.

[14] William J. Crowe, Assistant Director for Technical Services, personal communication to author.

[15] Heidi Lee Hoerman, *Technical Services Cost Studies in ARL Libraries* (Washington, D.C.: Association of Research Libraries, 1986), 22. I am grateful to Otha Overholt for bringing this item to my attention.

Part II
THE PRESENT SITUATION OF ACADEMIC LIBRARIANSHIP

4

Verner Clapp and Preservation of Library Materials
The Years at the Council on Library Resources

William J. Crowe

Verner Warren Clapp (1901-1972) was, in the words of his longtime friend and colleague William Dix, "close to the center of almost every important development in scholarly librarianship for at least 30 years." Dix included in his remarks at Clapp's memorial service a call for study of his life to "show what happened when a brilliant and imaginative mind was brought to bear on the current problems of an ancient profession in transition." The facts of Clapp's life have since been reported in standard biographical sources. Many of those librarians who know his name will associate Clapp with his long career at the Library of Congress, where he rose from the most junior ranks in the 1920s to become, in effect, the library's chief operating officer at mid-century, or with his subsequent leadership of the Council on Library Resources (CLR).

To understand Clapp and the continuing importance of his place in contemporary librarianship, however, one must also examine him in a context suggested by Dix—as "a genuine innovator, ... a splendid expositor and advocate."[1] Indeed, Clapp often described himself as a communicator. His career, especially in its last three decades, is clearly associated with change and the prospects for change in librarianship, if only because of the highly influential administrative positions that he held during contemporary American librarianship's "golden age."[2]

Clapp's almost half-century in libraries began in a time still rooted in practices developed at the the turn of the century, matured in the post-World War II period of great optimism about applications of scientific and technological knowledge, and ended only at the beginning of the age of computer applications. Many recognized the possibilities for change in American society, generally, and Clapp, among other leaders, saw opportunities to effect change in libraries, in particular. Of the several aspects of Clapp's work that exemplify his leadership in meeting the challenges of contemporary librarianship, examination of his role in early attempts to advance the cause of preservation of library materials provides special insight into the nature and *modus operandi* of his work as founding president of the CLR. The work of that organization, now entering its fourth decade, remains very much directed toward effecting change, and it is still closely involved with the complex of preservation issues that confront librarianship in the late twentieth century.

BEGINNINGS AT THE CLR

As the head of a body without precedent in librarianship, Clapp initially had only the most general of policy guidance on which to base decisions about initiatives that the CLR should take. The mission of the council had been stated succinctly in the news release issued by its benefactor, the Ford Foundation: "to support research and development of techniques and mechanisms that will help solve the acute problems of libraries."[3] The description of the new organization's intended activities and categories of probable expenditures restated, also in very general language, many of the issues discussed at two important meetings held in 1955 at the Folger Shakespeare Library, gatherings that the Ford Foundation had sponsored.[4] Clapp's own brief statement at the outset of the council's work, included in a background document offered to the press, had much the same quality:

> The aim of the Ford Foundation's grant to the Council, and the Council in its turn, is to attempt, without losing any of the values which libraries now contribute to our civilization, to make these values more accessible and more effective. Though there are few problems of libraries which money could not solve even with present procedures, it is quite unlikely that they will be solved that way. The aim of the Council is to bring concerted intelligence, as well as money, to these solutions.[5]

The first months of Clapp's work, beyond seeing to the essential tasks of establishing CLR's administrative operations, therefore had to be taken up with formulation of a concrete program. The Ford Foundation had conceived of the new agency not as a commission, as had been proposed after the Folger sessions, but rather as a council. It had been planned to bring together a group of knowledgeable men (no women were mentioned) who would function as links with other interests, as designers of a program, and as initiators of projects. They would do this with the assistance and advice of a secretariat, led by an experienced librarian-administrator, who, with other expert staff, would execute the program. Instead, CLR came into being functioning much like most traditional corporations or foundations, that is, with a strong administrator who was more knowledgeable about the field than many of the directors, and who took the lead in directing the organization. The board (the "council") was to be consulted on the setting of policy and asked to approve major projects. Several members of the council board confirmed, in confidence, to the Ford Foundation during its performance review of Clapp and the organization in 1960 that in the first years Clapp very much "had to operate almost alone."[6]

The council's early program and choice of projects to be funded were, then, very much Clapp's. He took the lead in identifying the challenges that required attention and in deciding how they should be attacked. For this, he could of course draw on the discussions of the earlier Folger meetings, in which he had been an active participant, and on his more than thirty years of professional experience. But here, Clapp's own interests also could be considered. Since Clapp was now freer to act than he had been at the Library of Congress, it is useful to review briefly Clapp's education and personal interests, the better to understand his choices for the council's attention.

Clapp had received a thoroughly classical undergraduate education. His degree program at Trinity College (Connecticut) was heavily weighted toward coursework in philosophy, English, Latin, Greek, and history. He took but two courses in the natural or physical sciences and mathematics.[7] In his personal interests, he was what is best described as a tinkerer, as he termed it, a "practitioner of the mechanic arts," and was in almost all things an enthusiast, eager to learn about almost everything around him, especially newly invented devices and improvements in methods of doing things. He always impressed his close associates and friends over the years with his delight in discovery. Put simply, Clapp insisted on knowing why and how things worked. This was true to the extent that during the last years of his life he noted and carefully recorded the results of his lungs' functioning to mark the progression of the emphysema that caused his death.

In these traits, Clapp may be seen as a part of an American tradition that saw technology as the driving force of progress. In the post-World War II era, especially, much of the nation's progress was being credited to the practical application of advances made in science and technology. Three concepts were central to this set of widely held beliefs: the need for research to produce new knowledge; the importance of systems of management based in scientific-engineering principles necessary to exploit new knowledge; and, ultimately, rapid and useful application of that knowledge.[8] This phenomenon reflects a view of science held by many American progressives of the early twentieth century, "science" being "practical knowledge and ability to manipulate the environment ... to respond ... to ... erupting social problems."[9] Clapp's initial decision, then, to categorize the council's first program as support of projects in basic research, technological development, and methodological development and coordination of effort very much reflects contemporary attitudes and beliefs about how American society's problems should be attacked.

Clapp was well aware of many of the challenges facing libraries and of the failures and shortcomings of most responses to them. His recommendation that work on preservation of library materials be the council's *third* major funded project was, however, a departure from the issues that had occupied much of his time at the Library of Congress. It is revealing to note how Clapp explained to the board and others the importance of moving ahead on so substantial a grant ($49,500) to the Virginia State Library for a study by William J. Barrow of the causes of and possible remedies for the deterioration of book paper. He especially had to justify this action in light of the council's first major award, $100,000 to Rutgers University (Ralph Shaw, project director), to identify the major issues facing libraries and the state of knowledge about them, the results of which were to be a major contribution to the setting of the CLR agenda. Clapp justified the almost simultaneous funding of the Barrow project, well in advance of any product from the Rutgers studies, as an opportunity to take immediate advantage of a recognized expert's

> enthusiasm ... [to bring] long[-]planned ... systematic investigations into paper deterioration on the hypothesis that this deterioration is due to causes which can be obviated in manufacture or arrested following manufacture at costs much less than those of any present process of document preservation.[10]

There can be little doubt that this initiative resulted to a degree from several years of informal discussions between Clapp and Barrow. Among the many congratulatory notes and letters that Clapp had received on his appointment as CLR's president was Barrow's. In this letter, Barrow also reported on a recent visit to the British Museum, where he had discussed with Frank Francis, Keeper of Printed Books, his prospects for "setting up a [laminating] shop" in London. Barrow had closed this letter by referring to his plans to see Clapp when he next visited Washington, the latest in a series of meetings that the two men had been having regularly since at least 1953.[11]

Clapp was very closely involved in the formulation of the proposal to fund Barrow's first CLR-sponsored project. Barrow reported to Francis on a long conference that he and Clapp had held in January 1957 to outline the proposal in detail, to settle on a home for the project, and to identify the specialists from the library and scientific communities who should serve as consultants. Barrow added in confidence that

> Verner is very enthusiastic about the plans ... and has intimated that this study, or similar ones, should be carried on for several years. I have found that he is not only interested in my project, but others that deal with all types of preservation and restoration in libraries.[12]

Clapp's acknowledgement to Randolph W. Church, State Librarian of Virginia and project administrator, of receipt of the finished proposal suggests that Barrow had not misread him: (April 19, 1957), "[an] investigation of the kind which you describe holds a great deal of interest for me personally and—I believe—has much importance." The proposal would be discussed by the council board that month.

Clapp's public statements of the time also began to include mention of the importance of preservation issues, especially the need to take action on problems of paper deterioration. For example, his remarks to a meeting on information retrieval in April 1957 included this long aside:

> Just a little help here might do a great many things in which we're all interested, like standardizing our specifications for ... materials that we use. Paper—the fact that it is effecting its deterioration and preservation. [sic] Perhaps just a little research here might give us a procedure by which we might rescue some of these deteriorating paper stocks. Perhaps just a little more organization might on the other hand make it unnecessary for us to have to accept in the future paper stocks which we will have in the future to protect from deterioration.[13]

FIRST WORK WITH BARROW
Adding to Knowledge and Mobilizing Interest

Despite Clapp's heavy commitments of time to other aspects of the CLR program—administration, preparation for meetings, and travel—he gave a great deal of his intellectual energy to issues of preservation, especially to Barrow and his work. Clapp and Barrow's working relationship was by then so well established that their correspondence regularly contained quite frank exchanges, such as Barrow's blunt criticism of the "restoration" section of Maurice Tauber's book, *Technical Services in Libraries* (New York: Columbia University Press, 1954). In the same letter Barrow also credited Clapp for substantial help with his own writing. "I now, more than ever," he wrote, "appreciate your assistance in writing my book [*Manuscripts and Documents: Their Deterioration and Restoration*]."[14]

The record of Clapp and Barrow's working relationship must be incomplete, as much of it was in informal personal meetings. It is evident, however, that Clapp and Barrow were in regular contact from the outset of work on "CLR-3," the council's designation for Barrow's first project, "Deterioration of Book-Stock—Causes and Remedies." They were both especially sensitive to the potential for challenge to this project by others, notably the paper industry. Clapp gave much advice to Barrow, particularly on how to avoid errors in procedure that might discredit knowledge produced by this project and the later (1959) "CLR-61" on "Improvement of Permanence/Durability of Book Papers."

The first communication to the library and publishing community about Barrow's council-funded work was Randolph Church's article, "Perish the Paper, Perish the Book, Perish the Thought: An Inquiry," which appeared in the September 3, 1957 issue of *Publisher's Weekly*. Clapp was also soon strongly urging Barrow to prepare an extended article explaining his findings to an audience that reached beyond the library and publishing world. He preferred a journal with a readership that included leaders in science and technology, people whose interest in preservation might be stimulated to the benefit of the cause. Clapp suggested *Science*. The result was the article, "Permanence in Book Papers," which appeared in the April 24, 1959 issue of *Science*, coauthored by Barrow and Reavis C. Sproull, one of his chemist-consultants. Barrow's files, however, show that Clapp also had a significant part in its writing. Clapp's first of three extended letters to Barrow on the manuscript of the article ran to four pages, including twenty-nine detailed questions and suggestions. In the end, Barrow once again expressed thanks to Clapp: "Now I can appreciate the vast amount of work that you have done on it."[15]

With Barrow's two early projects successfully completed, Clapp pressed ahead to advocate change by assembling, in September 1960, a group of leaders in librarianship and publishing. The meeting was called under the aegis of the American Library Association (ALA) and the Virginia State Library, with funding from the CLR. The conference was "to discuss the problems posed by deterioration of book papers, the formula developed by this [Barrow's] study and other possible solutions, and the implications involved."[16] Barrow could not attend the conference, but Clapp took an active part in its sessions. The report of the conference summarized the discussions and recorded an action that Clapp had hoped to obtain: a call to the ALA to establish a small working committee to develop producer-consumer support for promulgation of standards for permanent and durable book paper.

Within the week, Clapp wrote to Barrow, who had been in Europe on business, to describe the conference and especially to relate his earlier fear of its failure. He also was eager to start the process of change on other preservation issues.

> You will hear from Randy [Church] that the Conference on Permanent/Durable Paper, Washington, September 16, 1960, was a great success. It was, to an extent, Hamlet without Hamlet—it was a Conference on the Barrow paper without Barrow! This we all regretted, but made amends in some fashion by passing a resolution of commendation and gratitude to you.
>
> You will also learn from Randy that all parties were agreed to a continuation of consideration, and indicated their preparedness to be represented in a committee, to be convened by ALA, which will carry on by distributing information regarding development, suggesting further needed testing, etc.
>
> My own principal acquisition from the meeting was one of relief. I was never sure until the end of the meeting that there might not have been some time bombs waiting to be exploded in the form of either contempt for the whole business on the part of one or other of the groups, or the manifestation of intrenched and insoluble economic, technological, or regional problems. But none of these appeared. The whole attitude was one of considerable cooperation.
>
> Now there are several things which I would like to pursue with you. One of them is the matter of perfect binding, with respect to which you have sent me some suggestions, the consideration of which I deferred at the time. I am now anxious to get back to them.[17]

To build on Barrow's preservation work, Clapp next had to confront a basic problem in Barrow's lack of capital to establish a laboratory adequate to assume the intensive level of testing and research that the two men envisioned. Describing the state of his finances, Barrow reported to Clapp that he simply did not have the money, but he was eager to proceed. Clapp moved quickly to meet Barrow's need, discussing plans with him in February and March 1961 to develop a proposal for the CLR to fund the laboratory. The proposal, presented to the council's board on June 2, 1961, was for a two-year $125,000 grant. Clapp's written statement to the board stressed the need to add to the knowledge base for preservation and to test possible solutions:

> It has become increasingly clear over the past four years that Mr. Barrow has much to contribute to the Council's program. He combines the craftsman's feeling for materials with the historian's knowledge of their place in technological development; an urge for improvement; great ingenuity and inventiveness in effecting improvement; and an instinctive ability for complementing his own capabilities by the use of scientific advisers. He has, in one of the best-worked fields of technology, earned world-wide respect for his achievements.

In connection with the Council's work, he has been called upon not only in connection with the development of a permanent/durable paper, but also in connection with catalog card stock, testing of bookbindings, and adhesives. It appears probable that his services will be needed in connection with—among others—the ALA programs on bookbinding standards and quality control of book paper, and the work of the ARL Committee on Preservation of Library Materials.

Increasingly, too, it has become clear that such services could be rendered much more efficiently if Mr. Barrow had a laboratory for the purpose (his present laboratory is merely the manuscript repair shop of the Virginia State Library). If he could equip and staff a laboratory specifically for the purposes needed by the Council, much could be achieved in continuity and economy as well as in the better scheduling of his own time.[18]

While working to have Barrow's laboratory firmly established, Clapp began his own active work on three major preservation initiatives of the mid-1960s: the work of the ALA Committee on Permanent/Durable Paper (to which he and Barrow were named), the Committee on Preservation of Library Materials of the Association of Research Libraries (ARL), and preservation activity in the ALA Library Technology Project. In each instance, Clapp's strong advocacy for change is evident.

STALEMATE IN THE ALA COMMITTEE ON PERMANENT/DURABLE PAPER

Caution marked the start of the ALA-sponsored Committee on Permanent/Durable Paper, which had been called for at the September 1960 paper conference but did not get underway until January 1962, with Randolph Church as chairman. Clapp, who was formally added to the membership of the committee within a month of its start, was frank in his counsel to Church, seeking the best possible chance for change by seeking good relations with the representatives of the paper industry on the committee. He wrote:

The documents which have described the objectives of the Committee to date have emphasized the work of Bill Barrow. This is natural. We are all necessarily impressed by Bill's accomplishments. But in working with the industry we must be careful not to put ourselves into the position of pushing one man's work or one paper manufacturer's product.

Consequently, I think we should leave the name of Barrow out of the discussion for the immediate future, and emphasize—instead—the desirability of permanent-durable paper, no matter by what process made. Bill has proved that it can be done. Perhaps there are other methods besides. It is up to the industry to produce these other methods.[19]

After several frustrating meetings, however, Clapp was so stung by the uncooperative positions of some representatives of the paper industry on the committee that in July 1962 he vented his anger and dismay to Frazer Poole of the ALA Library Technology Project. " ... With respect to the permanent/durable paper question," he wrote, "we are in a den of wild animals."[20] By the following spring Barrow had also become so frustrated with the committee as to draft an exceedingly blunt memorandum for distribution to its members to set out the facts as he perceived them. Barrow, as he so often did, asked Clapp to comment on this draft. Clapp suggested that it would better achieve their objective if Clapp himself prepared an article for general distribution. Clapp's reasoning was as follows:

A. An article by me can put your permanent/durable paper development into historical perspective and can give you proper credit, which you yourself cannot do.

B. We badly need an article which will summarize the history of the development for those who are unaware of it, and even for those who (like the reviewer [Richard Shoemaker] of the LTP book on permanence and durability of catalog cards) suppose that the facts about deterioration have always been known and who consequently miss the significance of your researches.

C. Such an article would provide a neutral framework for the sermons which you want to preach, which otherwise might appear self-serving.[21]

Clapp's article appeared as " 'Permanent/durable' Book Papers," in *Library Journal* in October 1963.

Clapp's strategy throughout this episode reflected his usual desire to work effectively through such established collective authorities as the ALA Committee and, only after failing to achieve satisfactory results, to move ahead to identify or create other means to achieve his objectives. Even as he railed, in confidence, about the committee, Clapp urged caution to Barrow:

I have hopes that we may yet get some sweet reason out of the ... sub-committee and that this may affect the full Committee. If—contrary to my hope—[Harry F.] Lewis [a member of the committee representing the Institute of Paper Chemistry] and the Committee are recalcitrant, ALA or some other group may have to adopt its own specifications and conduct its own testing. But I would like first to give the Committee a chance to reach a consensus.[22]

The committee never did reach a consensus. The ARL withdrew its representative in 1966, and by 1968 the committee had dissolved because its members had arrived at a stalemate in technical subcommittee activities. Very much what Clapp had feared for the 1960 paper conference, deferral or rejection of action, had instead come to pass in the forum for action which that conference had recommended.

THE ARL COMMITTEE
Beginnings at Cooperation

Clapp's second attempt to influence a collective authority was to interest the member representatives of the ARL in preservation. He had alerted them to Barrow's findings (one copy of each of the first two Barrow reports was sent to each ARL library)—to prepare for ARL's participation at the September 1960 conference on paper, but more to encourage discussion of preservation at the June 1960 meeting of the association. At that meeting, Clapp, who was regularly invited to attend and participate in ARL meetings, described Barrow's work and the importance of developing performance-based specifications for book paper. There was extended general discussion about preservation problems, focusing more on existing library materials, and, in particular, on preservation microfilming. At the conclusion of the session, it was agreed that ARL should appoint a committee "to develop a national program for the preservation of research library materials with its primary concern directed toward the preservation of retrospective materials." Douglas Bryant of Harvard University was selected as chairman of this, the Committee on Preservation of Research Library Materials.[23]

Clapp became closely associated with the work of this committee from its beginning. Though he was not formally a member of the group, he attended and participated in many of its meetings. The committee depended heavily for its early work on information obtained from the Barrow studies, as well as on suggestions from Clapp that a careful study of the probable extent of deterioration of items in research library collections should be conducted, employing a sample of bibliographic records represented in the National Union Catalog. Clapp obtained council funding for this study, which was conducted by the Research Triangle Institute.[24]

The committee's second and overarching project, development of a national plan for preservation, was assigned in late 1962 to Gordon Williams, director of the Center for Research Libraries. The costs of the study were underwritten, again, by the council. The Williams report was issued in September 1964[25] and placed on the agenda for ARL's January 1965 meeting. Bryant, still chairman of the committee, reported that very few comments had been received from members in response to early distribution of the report. There was also only very limited discussion at the January session, William Dix supposing that "general unfamiliarity with a new concept" was the probable reason.[26] Clapp's more measured appraisal of Williams's work was that it was useful, but that the report was not adequate as a plan, in terms of concrete suggestions for action. He observed that Williams, despite the terms of the council grant, had not taken adequate time away from his work at the Center for Research Libraries to do the job adequately and that many technical questions were as yet unanswered.[27] Clapp did "not think there [was] a ghost of a likelihood that the federal government" [would] take over [Barrow's] kind of [research] operation," an important element of the Williams proposal.[28] Here, as at ALA, Clapp encountered in others a strong desire to defer action.

Clapp was instrumental in securing from the council funding needed to advance the third of the committee's projects of the mid-1960s. At the April 1966 meeting of the committee, he strongly urged support for a pilot project at the

Library of Congress "to explore the clerical procedures connected with preserving the 20,000 books represented by the [existing] brittle books coll[ection]."[29] The results of this project, which were reported to the committee and the council in late 1967, established the administrative feasibility of identifying and categorizing library materials needing preservation attention. The report did not, however, indicate what that attention should be, technically, or how such a program should be administered on a national scale.

THE LIBRARY TECHNOLOGY PROJECT AND LIBRARY BINDING

From the time of Clapp's early discussions and correspondence with Barrow on the permanent/durable paper question, he often mentioned as a central element of the preservation challenge the need to improve specifications for library binding and to develop an adhesive that could be used for perfect (i.e., glued, not sewn) binding without risk of early deterioration and destruction of a volume. Clapp had written to Barrow that although he had received a number of proposals to study binding, none of them was satisfactory "because of the deficiency of knowledge with respect to permanence."[30] Clapp met with Barrow several times during the winter of 1960-1961 to find a common focus of interest on binding, as well as to prepare for their participation in the ALA Committee on Permanent/Durable Paper.

Clapp's modus operandi here, as with the issue of permanent/durable paper, was to involve the ALA as fully as possible. In this case, he employed the good offices of the Library Technology Project (later Program) to administer a binding survey and study, with the aid of an advisory committee employing Barrow and his laboratory in the study phase.

The Library Technology Project (LTP) was created by the CLR with a grant to the ALA in December 1958 to meet one of the CLR's early stated objectives: promoting the testing and standardization of products associated with library work. One of LTP's early undertakings, the testing of the permanence/durability of catalog card stock, was assigned to Barrow in 1960. This effort concluded in 1961, but only after substantial difficulties between Barrow and LTP staff were resolved, with Clapp's personal intervention, on the content of the final report. Changes in the final report were requested by ALA's attorneys to avoid the appearance of endorsing any specific business or process, and this provoked Barrow to the point of suggesting that he could not undertake any future work administered by the LTP.[31]

Less than a month after that unpleasant experience, Clapp called together Barrow and Frazer Poole of LTP to devise a very specific plan, which Clapp subsequently summarized in four typewritten, single-spaced pages, for a two-year project to test the bindings of library books. Throughout, Clapp emphasized the need for communication, not only among the three of them but also with librarians and library binders. He also insisted that the *performance* of bindings under use should be the basis for new specifications, rather than accepting the previous focus on the quality of materials and "workmanship." Clapp felt strongly that "after Y circulations the case [of a book] should not be detached, the hinges not be broken, ... etc."[32]

The LTP/Barrow binding project and a Barrow study of the effects of aging on adhesives used in perfect binding, the latter administered directly by the council, both produced new knowledge. A useful testing apparatus was invented (the "universal book tester" and "openability plate"), and many of the study's findings were adopted by ALA and the Library Binding Institute. Again, however, Clapp had to intercede to keep Barrow and Forrest Carhart, Poole's successor in the LTP directorship, working together productively. Clapp attempted to explain Barrow's experiment to Carhart and stressed his high estimation of Barrow and his laboratory as "probably the most uniquely qualified ... for the development of performance standards for library binding in ... the world."[33]

The results of four years of work on the binding projects were summarized somewhat defensively by Barrow in 1965. His five-page letter to Clapp observed that "progress may have seemed slow, ... [but] worthwhile developments were made. In other words, ... a good beginning."[34] No performance standard for *permanence* had been achieved; owing to the many elements in bindings, their testing was much more complex than testing paper. Clapp's frustrations with the problems of binding led him to comment to Barrow that the effort "require[d] somewhat different auspices [i.e., not LTP] than it now has."[35] Clapp never was satisfied with this attempt to effect change, noting in 1967 that: "The 'Performance Standards for Library Bindings' exercise terminated, inconclusively for my taste. It was time, nevertheless, to terminate that particular exercise. ... I think we should have secured some such information for our $100,000."[36]

PRESERVATION OF MICROFILMING—EMPHASIS ON BIBLIOGRAPHIC CONTROL

During his tenure at the CLR, Clapp continued his substantial interest in the application of microphotography to library work, especially to advocate standardizing formats and improving equipment used to read and copy microforms. However, he openly questioned microform as a solution to problems of preservation, preferring instead to emphasize its importance for dissemination: "This is not to denigrate its [microform's] great importance as a preservative, as a copying medium, ... and various other things of this kind. But its great potential and still unexploited characteristic is as a medium of publication."[37] He wrote to Barrow, in typical candor:

> You can see for yourself what we are getting into with the proposals for microfilming all the books in United States libraries. Although this probably must be done eventually for other reasons than preservation (weeding of individual collections, central storage of films and photographic service on them) yet the fact remains that

there will be lots of books which individual libraries must keep in the original, regardless of the fact that there are microfilms in central collections. And besides, it'll be a long time before appreciable headway is made in microfilming all the books in all the libraries, considering that additions are made at the rate of a good many hundreds of thousands of separate items per year.[38]

Clapp, in his keynote address to the 1959 annual meeting of the National Microfilm Association, summed up his great optimism about the future of microforms, but emphasized that "until microforms can be made a personal accoutrement, as homely and as natural and as essential as the tooth-brush, the ball-point pencil, or as eyeglasses," they could not serve as replacements for the book.[39] Harking back to the concerns of many librarians and scholars, indeed to Louis Wright's own first call to the Ford Foundation that led to the calling of the Folger meetings, Clapp's emphasis in the area of preservation microphotography was to support the cooperative planning and coordination of copying projects. Along with Robert T. Jordan, he also reexamined the potential for use of microforms for storage of library materials, emphasizing issues of space utilization rather than of preservation.[40]

Clapp's longtime advocacy of more comprehensive bibliographic control for all library materials was evident in the council's support of Wesley Simonton's early study of bibliographic control of microforms.[41] Even more important was his advocacy for the council's providing funds in 1965 to enable the Library of Congress to establish an office to collect information for and to publish the *National Register of Microform Masters*, an indispensable tool for preservation purposes. Clapp's emphasis on the central importance of preservation microphotography based in coherent bibliographic control was clear. He felt that microreproduction had an important place in the preservation of records, but unless it was part of a well-planned program, it could be wasteful and therefore objectionable.[42]

His resistance to others' advocacy of some plans for preservation microfilming is evident in his response to efforts by University Microfilms to take the lead in a centralized program. In spring 1966, the ARL committee was presented with a proposal by Eugene Power, of University Microfilms, for a center for preservation microfilming, submitted in prompt response to the published version of the Williams report. Clapp shared the committee's negative reaction (Clapp described it in his notes: it "took a beating") to Power's proposal to have his company become *the* vehicle for a national preservation microfilming project.[43] Clapp was himself generally critical of University Microfilms, writing in 1969: "[University Microfilms'] success was no doubt merited; certainly libraries have greatly benefitted. ... However, the contribution ... has, in my view, been commercial and entrepreneurial in character rather than technological or bibliographic. As I have observed the operation over the years, ... its technology was provided by others and lagged rather than preceded, and the bibliographic know-how was similarly derived, typically from customers."[44]

LOOKING TO THE FUTURE
Institutionalizing Change

Clapp's middle years at the council, from 1963 through his retirement as its president in 1967, were marked by efforts to ensure the long-term continuation of its work, principally by incorporating elements of the program into the work of permanent organizations. From its beginnings, the council had been assured of financial support only for the term of awards from the Ford Foundation, initially for five years (1957-1961) and, on renewal in December 1960, for but an additional seven to ten years. Clapp was uncertain about the continued existence of the council, at least as he conceived of it and its work. He had been apprised during the last weeks of 1960 of the results of the Ford Foundation's initial review of the council and of his leadership, altogether a very positive appraisal, especially on Clapp's awareness of the environment: "Clapp and his staff were thoroughly up-to-date with what the Government and industry were doing. ... Clapp had regular liaison with all the agencies in the field."[45] But the Ford Foundation strongly emphasized the need for the council to give more attention to what its staff saw as the ultimate solution of library problems through mechanized storage and retrieval. The Ford Foundation board was advised by its staff that Clapp continued to be the leader of choice for this purpose: "Experience has now shown that the most informed point of contact between the computer man, the optics man and the scientific linguist, on the one hand, and the world of bibliographic storage and access, on the other, is the president of the Council on Library Resources."[46] Clapp's own view about "ultimate" solutions always would be less sanguine: "There is ... no single central problem of library work, and no single solution. Instead, advancement in the work as a whole results from improvement in details."[47]

Among the several pages of justification presented to the Ford Foundation in 1960 for continuation of funding for the council with Clapp at its head, it was noted that "one of the Foundation's consultants believes that ... [the Barrow paper projects] will result in savings far greater than any potential total investment by the Foundation in the Council, and many of the ... [Council] directors share this view." Throughout the review, however, the emphasis of the Ford Foundation's staff was decidedly *not* on preservation, but on the need for the council to focus more of its attention and resources on issues of storage and retrieval of information.[48]

It was nevertheless during these middle council years that Clapp also employed CLR's funding power to urge on and support the work of the Library of Congress with preservation, especially in response to the Williams report of 1964. The library's caution and Clapp's urging are adumbrated in Clapp's carefully worded version, in the council's eleventh annual report of the library's reaction to Williams's report. Clapp's principal attempt to shape the future of federal support for research and development on library problems, including attention to preservation, was by participating in the work of the National Advisory Commission on Libraries, to which he was appointed by President Johnson in 1966. Clapp, whose advice had often been solicited about who should serve on the commission, was now himself a member. His early recommendations to the others in the group emphasized both the "total library needs of the country" and the "principle that the consumer should have a voice in the control of national library services."⁴⁹ Clapp's twenty-one suggested recommendations for the commission's final report underscore these concerns and reflect much of what he had already stated in *The Future of the Research Library* (Urbana: University of Illinois Press, 1964), including two specific recommendations on preservation and a call for a broadly based program of research and development that echoed the CLR's own program.

During this period, Clapp also successfully urged CLR funding for the establishment and operation of a "Committee on Research Libraries," under the auspices of the American Council of Learned Societies, to advise the National Advisory Commission. That committee's work was summarized in its statement and recommendations submitted to the commission in November 1967.⁵⁰ The group's recommendations were similar to those made directly to the commission by Clapp, especially on the need for strong leadership by the federal government to move toward a coordinated national library policy. The committee's recommendations on preservation emphasized Barrow's work and the need for effective action to promote use of permanent/durable paper in book publishing. Clapp had a direct hand in this, having been asked by Thomas Brockway, the committee's staff director, to comment on a five-page statement by the U.S. Government Printing Office titled "Permanence of Printing Papers." In his response, Clapp faulted the statement, which had made no direct reference to Barrow or his findings, and which had mentioned Barrow indirectly only to suggest that his methods used in test-aging papers were suspect. Clapp helped to set straight the record, resulting in a clear statement by the commission of the problems of paper which credited Barrow's (and the CLR's) part in advancing a solution to those problems.⁵¹

THE LAST YEARS—RESEARCH AND EXHORTATION

Clapp's plans for retirement had included extended discussions with Barrow, who very much wanted Clapp to continue working closely with him. Barrow's conception of what Clapp's role might be is outlined in a letter he wrote to Clapp as he prepared to leave for Britain to consult on the quality of paper to be used in the publication of the *National Union Catalog* of pre-1956 imprints. Here, Barrow acknowledged most completely the part that Clapp had had, and could continue to have, in his work, principally as a communicator of knowledge and advocate for preservation. He wrote:

> 1. Your official position with this laboratory should be determined. Being a very active consultant would allow you almost complete freedom of operation, expression, etc. This type position deserves consideration.

2. You have been used continually as a librarian consultant and especially in the area of public relations and ethical practices. I continue to need this guidance.

3. Your advice relative to the needs of the librarian in relationship to research programs likewise should continue.

4. Assistance in the preparation of our reports and articles for publication are [sic] a need. You have exhibited the unique ability of conveying the thoughts of the scientist to the librarian. Few have this rare ability.

5. Your assistance in developing an acceptable budget for the Council and obtaining funds for the operation of this laboratory has been of inesteemable [sic] value. Your advice will be a need.

Many of the above relate primarily to a continuation of advisory services as a librarian. Your skill as a writer and ability to develop articles from data of this laboratory and printed sources is a great need.

I could go on and on because the needs of your services are multiple. The subject matter is like the many worthwhile projects we evaluate for this laboratory in that you and I see many more than can be done during our lifetime.[52]

Barrow's sudden death in August 1967 intervened, but even to the end, he and Clapp struggled to understand each other's sensibilities and values, as when Clapp cautioned Barrow in May 1967:

I think I detect a note of irritation in some of your recent answers. I can hardly blame you. However, let me remind you that this P/D V [the fifth volume in the Barrow series] is likely to constitute a landmark or classic in the study of paper. In any case it represents a very considerable investment of work. It is consequently important that it be written up the best way possible. I have invested many hours with this objective. If I fail to understand, I feel comparatively sure that my stupidity will be shared by other readers. Accordingly I ask your patience.[53]

Barrow had become very sensitive to what he viewed as denigration (or worse, ignorance) of his work by others in the field, especially governmental agencies. He also worried about being put out of business, as others began work on paper deterioration, to the extent that he prepared and sent to Clapp an *apologia*, an unpublished paper entitled "Investigations re: Acidity in Documents," which he hoped "some day ... [to] rewrite and publish ... to get the record straight."[54]

Clapp retired as president of the CLR in September 1967, but he retained among his responsibilities a half-time consultancy to CLR on its preservation-related projects. Much of his time in 1967 and 1968 was taken up in negotiating the continued operation of the Barrow Laboratory, a complex matter associated with settlement of Barrow's estate and resolution of the terms of the several contracts between Barrow and the council. During this process, for which Clapp had little patience, he summarized in frank confidentiality to Barrow's son Bernard his own part in Barrow's work, making clear that he had actively participated at several stages of the work in which Barrow was a principal figure.

> I should perhaps tell you something about my relationships with your Father, which were very far from being arms-length or bargaining relationships.
> I was at one time an amateur bookbinder, and acquired various responsibilities at the Library of Congress for the repair of documents (including supervision of the repair of the original of the Declaration of Independence), binding, and reference correspondence regarding preservation of library materials. It was natural that your Father and I should be thrown together. I gradually became his unofficial editor, and I have edited his publications (including those used in his repair business) for many years. I have spent many hundreds — yes many hundreds — of hours in very taxing business, and this, I have no doubt, has paid off in terms of spreading the Barrow gospel. I have never sought or desired recognition, acknowledgment or compensation in any form for this. The fact remains, however, that I have given substantially of time which might have been given to my own writing and research or other employments. So far from regretting this, I think it was a piece of good fortune that put my special talent at the service of his unique genius.
> While I was still at LC your Father and I used to discuss the need for research in the book-materials area. However, while I was able to throw small commissions his way, LC had no research money. But in 1956 I became president of the Council on Library Resources, Inc., and the road to research suddenly opened up. The rest is history.
> I do not mean to denigrate your Father's achievement in any way when I say that in the programs of research which he conducted with assistance from this Council we were a full, if a junior partner. We proposed topics of research, we followed the reports in detail, we made suggestions for improvements, alternative approaches, etc. This climate of active collaboration on a matter of mutual concern and excitement was, I am sure, as rewarding for your Father as it was to us.[55]

While Clapp strongly recommended that the council continue its support of the Barrow Laboratory, he recognized the need to sustain the process of change in preservation with the establishment of a permanent research and demonstration program. Promise of this finally appeared at the Library of Congress early in 1967, when Frazer Poole was appointed "preservation officer," with a mandate "to work not only with the Library's administrative and curatorial personnel but with ... national groups ... in a cooperative attack on preservation problems."[56]

In his years as president of the Council, Clapp had been largely frustrated in advancing the cause of preservation. He now looked to the Library of Congress and to Poole to take a leading role in continuing his work. In May 1967 he had written to Barrow:

> ... [T]here is no one in the library world capable of taking up the cudgels as you suggest [on behalf of research and development in preservation]. ... Frazer Poole may prove to be such a one. I had lunch with him ...; he enters into duties at LC on June 5, and must necessarily proceed cautiously. However, he fully expects to have a laboratory.[57]

The hoped-for laboratory, named the Preservation Research Office, was established at the Library of Congress in 1970, Clapp successfully recommending that the council provide financial support to help equip it. Clapp intended that the Barrow Laboratory's work continue for a time in parallel with that to be done at the new Library of Congress facility, but anticipated the probable demise of the Barrow operation.[58]

In retirement, Clapp had more time to focus his energies on topics of special personal interest, most notably the complex of issues associated with copyright and anticipated changes in U.S. copyright law, but he continued his interest in preservation. He followed developments in the field and displayed much interest in research conducted by Richard D. Smith, a doctoral student at the University of Chicago, on nonaqueous mass-deacidification of books. Clapp privately expressed some qualms about Smith's methods and what he saw as too close an association with the industry-oriented Institute for Paper Chemistry. Clapp saw no problem in Smith's basic line of investigation—indeed, he supported the council's providing him financial assistance. Nevertheless, he felt strongly that Smith had not given Barrow's work adequate credit and was concerned that Smith might be suggesting that success was close at hand, while Clapp still felt that much work, especially in persuading collective authority to act, was yet to be done. He cautioned about "leading people to think that success is right around the corner, and the next, and the next, and the next."[59]

In Clapp's view, much progress had been made. Much technical knowledge had become available or was being developed by researchers; a body of preservation literature was well begun, including a new international journal, *Restaurateur*, with Clapp on its editorial board; and the outline of a national plan (the Williams report) had been accepted in principle by the collective of research libraries. What Clapp felt was most needed next was to adopt and implement a broad, national plan of action. This crucial step in the process of change had eluded him.

In 1968 Warren J. Haas, director of libraries at the University of Pennsylvania, became the new chairman of the ARL Committee on Preservation of Research Library Materials. He was, in Clapp's words, prepared to take "the bull by the horns," by proposing to the committee an early comprehensive review of the state-of-the-preservation-art by a disinterested entity such as Arthur D. Little, Inc., which could then recommend action that needed to be taken. Clapp was more than supportive. "Even if you lead him [the bull] into a china shop, this is preferable to letting him repose on his fanny!" he wrote, but he was doubtful about introducing a new player into the process. "We would ... spend a lot of money educating ... [a consulting firm] before commencing to get results," he opined, preferring instead "to repeat the previous performance (with Gordon Williams) by employing someone who already knows where to look and what the problems are."[60]

In April 1970, as a result of the revived ARL committee's work, the ARL requested funds from the U.S. Office of Education "for the development of specifications for a national plan ... [to] include ... administrative, operational and bibliographic organization,"[61] to be led by Haas, a man who presumably knew where to look, with project assistance drawn from ARL's own staff. The product of this study, completed after Clapp's death, was a comprehensive planning document that emphasized coordinated national action on preservation,[62] with a leading part to be taken by the Library of Congress.

Clapp was able, despite worsening health problems, to devote more of his time and energy in retirement to communicating his opinion about the need to act on and to disseminate information about preservation. In a speech at the New York Library Association's Conference on Preservation of Materials in November 1970, he told the story from which came his article "The Declaration of Independence: A Case Study in Preservation."[63] Much of his last energy also went for the first time directly into personal research on preservation for the much-praised series of three articles entitled "Story of Permanent/Durable Book Paper, 1115-1970."[64]

Clapp's last comment on preservation came in "LTP—The Rattle in an Infant's Fist," published posthumously in the July/August 1972 issue of *American Libraries*. This article is both a recounting of the short history of the Library Technology Project/Program and a capsule history of applications of technology to library work. Clapp highlighted both LTP's failures and such successes as its Se-Lin book-labeling device and Barrow's work on testing and establishing standards for permanence/durability of catalog cards. He also underscored work that LTP had successfully concluded but that had not as yet been applied successfully to library problems. In discussing his frustrations with LTP's work on bookbinding, he issued his final call for action on preservation. "Although this work broke new ground and created new information," he reminded his readers that "it needs to be picked up again and carried further."[65]

CONCLUSIONS

The challenge of effecting change in the preservation of library materials is unarguably herculean, and was recognized as such by Clapp. He insisted that the many problems that make up this challenge would require attention over many years before effective change could be seen, a judgment that has been borne out by events. The strategies that he used to promote change in preservation have been continued by the succeeding generation of library leaders, a good example being the Council on Library Resources' sponsorship of the Committee on Production Guidelines for Book Longevity, established in 1979 as a means to draw together several interest groups. Its basic objectives, given advances in knowledge since the early 1960s, were not too far removed from those of the ALA Committee proposed on paper at the 1960 conference.[66]

As Clapp commented soon after the council had begun its work, he saw his primary responsibility to be the relation of "the rarified atmosphere of mathmatical [sic] analysis to the smoke-filled room of economics, politics, and administration," to marry "the arts of reason to those of persuasion."[67] Clapp's work reflected and benefited from these qualities, especially as he sought to meet the many challenges of preservation. He lived a full intellectual life in the study of philosophy, history, languages, and bibliography; experienced firsthand the tools and methods of the workbench; and developed a remarkable talent for gaining and keeping the esteem and trust of others. The combination of these qualities—of the scholar, the practitioner/tinkerer, and the politician—place Clapp very much in the domain of the advocate and innovator so necessary to advance a cause. Clapp was responding, in effect, as he apparently did in so many areas, to his good friend Luther Evans's strong admonition: "Verner, do something; do you want [libraries] ... to fail because of your lack of leadership?"[68]

NOTES

[1]William S. Dix, in *Verner Warren Clapp, 1901-1972: A Memorial Tribute* (Washington, D.C.: Library of Congress, 1973), 6.

[2]George S. Bobinski, "The Golden Age of American Librarianship," *Wilson Library Bulletin* 58 (January 1984): 338-44.

[3]Council on Library Resources, Inc., untitled news release, dated September 18, 1956, David C. Mearns Papers, Box 73, Library of Congress, Washington, D.C.

[4]Cf. "Report on Conference on Problems of Acquisition, Preservation, and Dissemination of Library Materials," Folger Shakespeare Library, Washington, D.C., 1955 (typescript) and "Minutes of a Conference on Library Problems, Held at the Folger Library, March 31, 1955," Folger Shakespeare Library, Washington, D.C., 1955 (typescript).

[5]Council on Library Resources, Inc., "Background Data on the Formation of Council on Library Resources, Inc." September 18, 1956 (typescript), David C. Mearns Papers, Box 73, Library of Congress, Washington, D.C.

[6]W. McNeil Lowry to Records Center, Memorandum, August 12, 1960, Council on Library Resources Files, Ford Foundation Archives, PA56-0219, New York.

[7]Transcript of Verner W. Clapp, Trinity College. Clapp took twenty-eight courses at Trinity: five in philosophy, seven in English, two in French, two in Latin, five in Greek, three in history, and one each in first level mathematics, geology, economics, and German.

[8]Julius A. Stratton, *Science and the Educated Man: Selected Speeches of Julius A. Stratton* (Cambridge: MIT Press, 1966), 90.

[9]Ronald C. Tobey, *The American Ideology of National Science, 1919-1930* (Pittsburgh: University of Pittsburgh Press, 1971), 18.

[10]Council on Library Resources, Inc. *1st Annual Report for the Period Ending June 30, 1957* (Washington, D.C.: Council on Library Resources, 1957), 21-22. See also the extended review of the council's early involvement with preservation in Nancy E. Gwinn, "CLR and Preservation," *College and Research Libraries* 42 (March 1981):104-26 and Pamela W. Darling and Sherelyn Ogden, "From Problems Perceived to Programs in Practice: The Preservation of Library Resources in the U.S.A., 1956-1980," *Library Resources & Technical Services* 25 (January/March 1981): 9-29.

[11]William J. Barrow to Verner W. Clapp, letter, October 31, 1956, Barrow Correspondence File, Council on Library Resources, Washington, D.C.

[12]Barrow to Frank C. Francis, letter, January 25, 1957, Correspondence File, William J. Barrow Papers, Virginia Historical Society, Richmond, Va.

[13]Verner W. Clapp, Notes for speech at the Symposium for Systems for Informational Retrieval, Western Reserve University, April 18, 1957, Verner W. Clapp Papers, Box 43, Library of Congress, Washington, D.C.

[14]Barrow to Clapp, letter, November 3, 1954, Correspondence File, William J. Barrow Papers, Virginia Historical Society, Richmond, Va.

[15]Barrow to Clapp, letter, March 26, 1959, "CLR-Correspondence" File, William J. Barrow Papers, Virginia Historical Society, Richmond, Va.

[16]*Permanent/Durable Book Paper; Summary of the Conference Held in Washington, D.C.* (Richmond: Virginia State Library, 1960), 27-28. (The Barrow studies had been reported in *Deterioration of Book Stock, Causes and Remedies: Two Studies on the Permanence of Book Paper Conducted by W.J. Barrow* [Richmond: Virginia State Library, 1959]).

[17]Clapp to Barrow, letter, September 22, 1960, "CLR-Correspondence" File, William J. Barrow Papers, Virginia Historical Society, Richmond, Va.

[18]"A Laboratory for Research in Book Materials," Council Board Review 61-1, June 2, 1961, Barrow Files, Council on Library Resources, Washington, D.C.

[19]Clapp to Randolph W. Church, letter, February 9, 1962, Verner W. Clapp Papers, Box 15, Library of Congress, Washington, D.C.

[20]Clapp to Frazer G. Poole, letter, July 9, 1962, Verner W. Clapp Papers, Box 15, Library of Congress, Washington, D.C.

[21] Clapp to Barrow, letter, May 24, 1963, "CLR-Correspondence" File, William J. Barrow Papers, Virginia Historical Society, Richmond, Va.

[22] Clapp to Barrow, letter, October 18, 1963, Barrow Correspondence File, Council on Library Resources, Washington, D.C.

[23] Association of Research Libraries, *Minutes of the 55th Meeting* (Washington: Association of Research Libraries, 1960), 6-7.

[24] "Magnitude of the Paper-Deterioration Problem As Measured by a National Union Catalog Sample," *College & Research Libraries* 23 (November 1962):499; 543.

[25] *The Preservation of Deteriorating Books: An Examination of the Problem with Recommendations for a Solution* (Washington, D.C.: Association of Research Libraries, 1964). Williams prepared two articles based on the report: "The Preservation of Deteriorating Books: Part I: An Examination of the Problem," *Library Journal* 91 (January 1, 1966):51-56 and "The Preservation of Deteriorating Books: Part II: Recommendations for a Solution," *Library Journal* 91 (January 15, 1966):189-94.

[26] Association of Research Libraries, *Minutes of the 65th Meeting* (Washington, D.C.: Association of Research Libraries, 1965), 3. Carolyn Morrow, describing this episode in preservation history, drew other conclusions: "The proposal went over like a lead balloon. ... Money was easy, and libraries were intent on building collections. So what if a few dusty volumes lay crumbling?" (Carolyn Clark Morrow, "National Preservation Planning and Regional Cooperative Conservation Efforts," in *Conserving and Preserving Library Materials*, eds. Kathryn Luther Henderson and William T. Henderson [Urbana-Champaign, Ill.: Graduate School of Library and Information Science, University of Illinois, 1983], 37).

[27] Clapp to Warren J. Haas, letter, December 6, 1968, Verner W. Clapp Papers, Box 18, Library of Congress, Washington, D.C.

[28] Clapp to Barrow, letter, April 20, 1965, "CLR-Correspondence" File, William J. Barrow Papers, Virginia Historical Society, Richmond, Va.

[29] Verner W. Clapp, notes taken at April 29, 1966 meeting of the ARL Committee on Preservation of Research Library Materials, Verner W. Clapp Papers, Box 18, Library of Congress, Washington, D.C.

[30]Clapp to Barrow, letter, December 17, 1960, "CLR-Correspondence" File, William J. Barrow Papers, Virginia Historical Society, Richmond, Va.

[31]Barrow to Frazer G. Poole, letter, September 1, 1961 and Clapp to Barrow, letter, September 6, 1961, Barrow Correspondence File, Council on Library Resources, Washington, D.C.

[32]Clapp to Frazer G. Poole, letter, September 19, 1961, "CLR-Correspondence" File, William J. Barrow Papers, Virginia Historical Society, Richmond, Va.

[33]Clapp to Forrest F. Carhart, letter, April 23, 1964, "CLR-Correspondence" File, William J. Barrow Papers, Virginia Historical Society, Richmond, Va.

[34]Barrow to Clapp, letter, August 4, 1965, "CLR-Correspondence" File, William J. Barrow Papers, Virginia Historical Society, Richmond, Va. The two reports issued were: *Development of Performance Standards for Library Binding, Phase I: Report of the Survey Team*, LTP Publications, no. 2 (Chicago: American Library Association, 1961) and *Development of Performance Standards for Binding Used in Libraries, Phase II: Report on a Study Conducted by the Library Technology Project*, LTP Publications, no. 10 (Chicago: American Library Association, 1966).

[35]Clapp to Barrow, letter, August 3, 1965, "CLR-Correspondence" File, William J. Barrow Papers, Virginia Historical Society, Richmond, Va.

[36]Clapp to Jean Karl, letter, November 17, 1967, Verner W. Clapp Papers, Box 19, Library of Congress, Washington, D.C.

[37]Verner W. Clapp, quoted in *Libraries and Automation: Proceedings of the Conference on Libraries and Automation* (Washington, D.C.: Library of Congress, 1964), 148-49.

[38]Clapp to Barrow, letter, January 31, 1961. "CLR-Correspondence" File, William J. Barrow Papers, Virginia Historical Society, Richmond, Va.

[39]Verner W. Clapp, notes for keynote address to the National Microfilm Association, April 2, 1959, Verner W. Clapp Papers, Box 43, Library of Congress, Washington, D.C.

[40]Verner W. Clapp and Robert T. Jordan,"Re-evaluation of Microfilm as a Method of Book-storage," *College & Research Libraries* 24 (January 1963):5-15.

[41]Wesley Simonton, "The Bibliographical Control of Microforms," *Library Resources & Technical Services* 6 (Winter 1962):29-40.

42Council on Library Resources, Inc., *9th Annual Report* (Washington, D.C.: Council on Library Resources, 1965), 23.

43Verner W. Clapp, notes taken at April 29, 1966 meeting of the ARL Committee on Preservation of Research Library Materials, Verner W. Clapp Papers, Box 18, Library of Congress, Washington, D.C.

44Verner W. Clapp to Admissions Committee, Cosmos Club, letter on E. Power, January 10, 1969, Verner W. Clapp Papers, Box 27, Library of Congress, Washington, D.C.

45W. McNeil Lowry to Records Center, Memorandum, September 26-28, 1960, p. 23, Council on Library Resources Files, Ford Foundation Archives, PA56-0219, New York.

46"Excerpt from Docket of Ford Foundation Board of Trustees Meeting of December 8, 1960," Council on Library Resources Files, Ford Foundation Archives, PA56-0219, New York.

47Council on Library Resources, Inc., *10th Annual Report* (Washington, D.C.: Council on Library Resources, 1966), 15-16.

48"Excerpt from Docket of ... December 8, 1960," 5.

49Clapp to Melville J. Ruggles, letter, February 9, 1967, Verner W. Clapp Papers, Box 32, Library of Congress, Washington, D.C.

50*On Research Libraries: Statement and Recommendations of the Committee on Research Libraries of the American Council of Learned Societies* (Cambridge, Mass.: MIT Press, 1969).

51Clapp to Thomas P. Brockway, letter, August 1, 1967, Verner W. Clapp Papers, Box 35, Library of Congress, Washington, D.C.

52Barrow to Clapp, letter, June 12, 1967, "CLR-308" Files, Council on Library Resources, Washington, D.C.

53Clapp to Barrow, letter, May 26, 1967, "CLR-318" Files, Council on Library Resources, Washington, D.C.

54In "CLR-308" File, Council on Library Resources, Washington, D.C.

55Clapp to Bernard G. Barrow, letter, August 19, 1968, "CLR-429" File, Council on Library Resources, Washington, D.C.

⁵⁶*Library of Congress Information Bulletin* 26 (March 9, 1967):178-79.

⁵⁷Clapp to Barrow, letter, May 15, 1967, "CLR-308" File, Council on Library Resources, Washington, D.C.

⁵⁸Clapp to Fred Cole, memorandum, July 1, 1971, "CLR-460" File, Council on Library Resources, Washington, D.C.

⁵⁹Clapp to Robert N. DuPuis, letter, March 1, 1971, "CLR-460" File, Council on Library Resources, Washington, D.C.

⁶⁰Clapp to Warren J. Haas, letter, December 6, 1968, Verner W. Clapp Papers, Box 18, Library of Congress, Washington, D.C.

⁶¹"Office of Education Supports ARL Study of a National System for the Preservation of Library Materials," news release, April 22, 1970, Verner W. Clapp Papers, Box 18, Library of Congress, Washington, D.C.

⁶²Warren J. Haas, *Preparation of Detailed Specifications for a National System for the Preservation of Library Materials* (Washington, D.C.: Association of Research Libraries, 1972).

⁶³Verner W. Clapp, "The Declaration of Independence: A Case Study in Preservation," *Special Libraries* 62 (December 1971):503-08.

⁶⁴Verner W. Clapp, "Story of Permanent/Durable Book Paper, 1115-1970," *Scholarly Publishing* 2 (January-July 1971):107-24; 229-45: 353-67.

⁶⁵Verner W. Clapp, "LTP—The Rattle in an Infant's Fist," *American Libraries* 3 (July-August 1972):800.

⁶⁶The Committee's work led to publication of *Book Longevity: Reports of the Committee on Production Guidelines for Book Longevity* (Washington, D.C.: Council on Library Resources, 1982). The Committee's work was also instrumental in approval of the *American National Standard for Information Sciences—Permanence of Paper for Printed Library Materials* (New York: American National Standards Institute, 1985).

⁶⁷Verner W. Clapp, notes for remarks made at the opening of the International Conference on Scientific Information, November 16, 1958, Verner W. Clapp Papers, Box 29, Library of Congress, Washington, D.C.

⁶⁸"Memo to Clapp from Evans," January 1, 1954, Verner W. Clapp Papers, Box 6 and Box 18, Library of Congress, Washington, D.C.

5

Faculty Status of Librarians
A Comparative Study of Two Universities in the United Kingdom and How They Compare to the Association of College and Research Libraries Standards

James L. Mullins

In the United States, the issue of faculty status for librarians in an institution of higher education has been an important concern for at least the past quarter century. This issue arose when it became apparent to librarians that they did not have a logical niche within the university's administrative structure. Were the librarians professionals, academics, support staff, administrative personnel, or faculty? The question has been answered over the years in many different ways; each institution of higher education has addressed it differently, responding in its own manner and in its own way.

In order to bring some uniformity to the situation, the Association of College and Research Libraries (ACRL), in 1972, adopted standards by which librarians were to be judged to determine if they had achieved faculty status. The standards, which were developed with concern for librarians in the United States, include: (1) professional responsibilities and self-determination, (2) library governance, (3) college and university governance, (4) compensation, (5) tenure, (6) promotion, (7) leaves, (8) research funds, (9) academic freedom.[1]

More recently the relationship of librarians to their parent institutions has become an issue in other countries. Do librarians outside the United States view their relationship to the institution in which they work differently? Specifically, what has been the experience of librarians in the United Kingdom?

Using the case study method, this investigation examines two universities, Oxford University and the University of Bristol. These universities represent the two major types of postsecondary institutions in the United Kingdom. Although the results of this study cannot be considered definitive of the status of librarians in the United Kingdom, it will give American librarians the opportunity to judge whether British librarians at two different British universities have developed a unique relationship with their university or whether their relationship is in agreement with the provisions as stated in the ACRL standards.

LITERATURE REVIEW

Two excellent articles that surveyed the literature on faculty status during the past twenty years appeared in the professional literature during the spring of 1987. These articles not only provide an excellent overview of the findings of various surveys conducted during this period, but they also describe some of the attitudes that have arisen about faculty status in the United States.

Emily Werrell and Laura Sullivan, in their article "Faculty Status for Academic Librarians: A Review of the Literature,"[2] only surveyed the literature concerning the status of librarians in the United States. They covered the period from the mid-1970s through 1985, up to the time when librarians began to ask questions about the desirability of faculty status. What was the impetus to develop the guidelines on faculty status, as approved by the ACRL, the American Association of University Professors and the Association of American Colleges? Werrell and Sullivan believe it "hinged primarily upon librarians' image of themselves as educators, with scholarly interests and knowledge on a par with those of the teaching faculty."[3]

Werrell and Sullivan found varying levels of success in achieving the nine criteria used to determine if a librarian had true faculty status. One of the criteria, governance and collegiality, seemed to be the point on which most librarians believed they had reached parity with their teaching faculty colleagues. They were least comparable with their teaching faculty colleagues on the issue of salary and benefits.

The review of surveys undertaken by Krompart and DiFelice[4] was informative regarding the attitudes librarians held about their role in the university. The researchers report on some surveys that evaluate how well the librarians fulfilled their assigned mission on the campus. A critical point made by the authors, after reviewing the surveys undertaken between 1971 and 1984, was that "one right or responsibility carries another, and a change in one condition seems likely to have an impact on several."[5] This statement is significant; it seems to imply that if librarians are recognized as members of the senate or given faculty rank, they will be more likely to achieve parity on the other criteria as well since in the minds of the faculty they are viewed as colleagues.

It is easy to determine from the two reviews that librarians still cannot quite decide under which system they are best served and recognized. Another factor, which Krompart and DiFelice isolated and which has significance for librarians trying to achieve faculty status in the United States, is "employment in a large public institution appears to be the circumstance most likely to contribute to higher incidence of conditions and responsibilities in line with the Standards."[6]

Although the literature has not been as extensive on the status of academic librarians in the United Kingdom, some significant developments concerning the conditions of academic librarians have occurred there. In 1964 the Association of University Teachers stated in a report: "It must be recognized once and for all that university libraries provide an absolutely fundamental service which affects the whole university and without which it would cease to function as a centre for teaching and research."[7] This quote does not make any statement about the contractual relationship of the librarians to the university. It does, however, state the basis on which librarians can argue for their unique and essential role in the educational process, thereby setting the stage for their request for faculty status recognition.

In 1978 the Library Association published a policy which stated the following:

> The Association reiterates most forcefully its view that the senior members of the library staff must be recognized as being in all respects an integral part of the academic life of the institution and must be appropriately incorporated into its structure in terms of status, salaries, and conditions of service.[8]

The Library Association was recommending that only librarians in the higher levels of administration (i.e., senior members) should be granted faculty status. Faculty status is not automatically given to a librarian upon entering a position classified as professional. Unlike the United States, where most professional library positions require a master's degree in library science, the United Kingdom is much more flexible in its requirements. Often a specialized degree is more crucial to securing a library position than formal training in library and information science.

More recently an interesting distinction has been evident in the literature, that of the scholar librarian or the "academic" librarian. This person has been defined in various ways, but most often as the librarian who has the closest contact with the academic departments and who serves as a liaison between these departments and the library. Dr. F.W. Ratcliffe, University Librarian of Cambridge University, in a recent interview stated that "a scholar librarian to me is a librarian with a disciplined mind; he is not a person who is stuffed up to the eyeballs with Ph.D.s and research degrees, ... he is a person who takes a disciplined interest in his work and in his profession."[9]

CASE STUDIES

During May and June of 1987, the author attended the Seminar on English Librarianship sponsored by Oxford University's Bodleian Library and the University of Oklahoma. This seminar allowed its participants to study and research aspects of English librarianship. It included presentations by library administrators, educators, and professional library staff members. It also presented opportunities to visit with and follow up on questions raised by the presentations. The scope of the seminar was quite broad, but it was possible for members to narrow the focus on their own and direct their attention to particular aspects of English librarianship.

I chose to study two particular libraries in depth: the Bodleian at Oxford University and the University Libraries at the University of Bristol. The observations gained from these two libraries may be typical of the particular type of library each represents. The Bodleian at Oxford represents those libraries with long histories such as Cambridge, Edinburgh, or Trinity. These universities, steeped in tradition and protocol, are quite different from those often referred to as the "Red Brick Universities." The University of Bristol represents the latter type of institution. The relationship of the librarians to the university will be reviewed in each institution.

The Bodleian Library of Oxford University is, of course, one of the oldest university libraries in the world. Founded in 1488 by a bequest of Duke Humphrey, brother of Henry V, the library was begun with a collection of 400 manuscripts. It was not long before this library was overshadowed by the development of college libraries that were avidly collecting printed books, which, to the college student, had more practical application than the older manuscripts. After the decline in use of the library, due to the impact of the printed books and the growth of the college libraries, the final blow came to the original Bodleian Library when Henry VIII, through his zeal to reform the church, caused the collection to be either destroyed or scattered. It was not until Sir Thomas Bodley decided the goal of his life would be to rebuild the library at Oxford University that the library known today came into being.

Bodley purchased books and commissioned buyers to travel around Europe to purchase items for him. Bodley also hired the librarian. To this day, the chief administrator of the library is referred to as Bodley's Librarian. In 1608 Bodley secured the copyright privilege which required that a copy of every book published in Britain be deposited with the library at no charge to the library. This arrangement has ensured a complete record of English publishing since the early seventeenth century. Later, the depository program was extended to include Cambridge and eventually six other libraries throughout the United Kingdom.

The Bodleian Library is a representative of a comprehensive academic library collection, but along with this comes a heritage of 300 years. One part of that history is the status of the librarian within the library and the university.

The University of Bristol, which was included as part of the seminar, allowed the opportunity to study and analyze its library. The "Red Brick Universities" were created by Parliament in the mid-nineteenth century to serve the major population and industrial centers of Britain. These universities, somewhat analogous to our state universities, brought higher education to a broader spectrum of the British population. Although such universities as Leeds, Sheffield, Manchester, and Bristol do not have the history associated with Oxford or Cambridge, they have grown to be major research universities. Unlike Oxford, a university such as Bristol is not overly encumbered by traditions, rules, and regulations reaching back three centuries. Does this mean the librarians at Bristol have a different role or different rights within the university than their colleagues at Oxford?

A significant factor in examining the status of librarians within the university community in the United Kingdom is the process by which a librarian is professionally qualified. The Library Association certifies individual librarians by reviewing their credentials and granting them either a designation of Associate, Library Association (ALA) or as a Fellow, Library Association (FLA). This "certification" does not depend upon completion of a library school program but can be granted to staff members trained in other fields who have come to librarianship without formal library education.

The relatively recent development of formal university library education is one of the reasons why a greater interest in faculty status has not developed on the part of the librarians. The first library school was begun in 1919 at the University of London. Other library schools did not appear until the 1950s. Many of the college and university librarians in the United Kingdom came to be librarians through the apprenticeship route more typical of the United States in the nineteenth century. It was common for a faculty member to be moved from an academic department to the library. Often faculty members had dual responsibility for the library and teaching. The "Librarian," therefore, by tradition was considered a member of the faculty, while the other librarians were seen as his helpers or assistants with little formal education. With the advent of formal library school training, the assistant librarians became more skilled.

CRITERIA

The criteria that will be used to evaluate the status of librarians at the Bodleian Library at Oxford University and the librarians at the University of Bristol will be the "Faculty Status Standards" as approved by the ACRL. These standards have been used as a guideline for librarians in the United States and are still the measure by which librarians determine whether they have achieved faculty status within their institutions. The information collected from the two libraries was primarily obtained through personal interviews and lectures which were part of the seminar. Follow-up was accomplished through correspondence with Bodley's Librarian and with the University Librarian at Bristol.

Professional Responsibilities and Self-Determination. At Oxford and Bristol, it was clear both through discussions with David Vaisey, Bodley's Librarian at Oxford, and Norman Higham, Director of Libraries, University of Bristol, and with various staff members of the library, that self-determination in their work was a fact. The librarians had direction as to their responsibilities in the library, but were left to accomplish their objectives on their own. The classification of the library staff in each institution showed evidence of an understanding of what was expected of a professional.

A peer review committee does not exist at either Oxford or Bristol. Vaisey[10] and Higham[11] both stated that a staff evaluation may soon be introduced nationally by the government. Since both institutions are government-funded, standards for personnel are devised by the government and apply to both universities as well as the other state-supported institutions of higher education. Higham further stated that reviews are "being introduced throughout the University for academic and academic-related staff (including Assistant Librarians and above)."[12]

Library Governance. On this point Oxford and Bristol diverge. Although neither has a body referred to as an administrative council, each has an advisory body that suggests or recommends policy decisions; however, their oversight differs as described below.

Bodley's Librarian holds an officers' meeting. This group consists of the Keepers of Printed Books, of Western Manuscripts, of Oriental Books and Manuscripts, and of Scientific Books, together with the Secretary of the Library.[13] This body represents the heads of the four departments into which the library is divided. Bodley's Librarian chairs the meeting. The committee discusses and advises Bodley's Librarian on all aspects of library policy and administration.[14] But the final policy is set by the Curators (governing body) of the library, as advised by Bodley's Librarian after consultation with participants of the officers' meeting.[15] The Curators of the library are members of the university faculty and are somewhat analogous to what is often known in American universities as the Faculty Library Committee.

At Bristol, there is no administrative council; however, there is a staff committee which represents the eighty-seven full-time equivalent staff members. This committee consists of all librarians with the rank of Assistant Librarian and above as well as a representative from each of the Senior Library Assistants (Main Library), Senior Library Assistants (Branches), Library Assistants (Main Library), Library Assistants (Branches), and Secretarial and Clerical staff. The committee meets at least three times a year to discuss problems, procedures, and policy, when appropriate. It also receives reports from the Librarian and from the Library Committee.[16] The library committee is composed of representatives from the various faculties.

Oxford and Bristol have titular designations to differentiate the various educational qualifications of the librarians and their experience levels. The title given library staff members to some degree also relates to their status or responsibility within the library. At Oxford, there are four grades for professional librarians, starting with the highest: Officers, Principal Assistant Librarians, Senior Assistant Librarians, and Assistant Librarians. The only required academic qualification is a first degree (the undergraduate bachelor degree), but other degrees (e.g., subject master's or doctorate) may be requested, depending upon the position. Librarians do not have academic status; they are what is referred to as "academic related."[17]

At Bristol, the librarians are divided into the ranks of: Librarian, Deputy Librarian, Sub-Librarians, Assistant Librarians. All of these positions are expected to have a "good honors degree"[18] —a bachelor's degree denoting that the student ranked in the upper 25 percent of the class—as well as professional library qualifications. Senior library assistants are expected to have library experience but not be professionally qualified. Academic status at Bristol implies membership in the university.[19] This status is restricted to the teaching faculty of the university. Of library staff only the Librarian has academic status, since he or she is the only library member of the Senate. The Librarian also has the honorific title of Special Lecturer in Bibliography.[20]

College and University Governance. At Oxford, the librarians have various designations to indicate their relationship to the university. Vaisey states:

"Academic" standing is achieved in three ways:

 i. Membership of Congregation: the assembly of resident Masters and Doctors of the University—the ultimate voting body for university legislation.

 ii. Membership of a Faculty (of, say, Modern History, or Clinical Medicine)—the body which controls the curriculum and teaching in that subject.

 iii. A Fellowship at a College.

To take these in order:

 i. Librarians achieve Membership of Congregation when they reach a fixed point on the salary scale for Assistant/Senior Assistant Librarians; and provided that they are MAs of Oxford University or have equivalent qualifications of another university which give them "MA status" of Oxford.

 ii. Membership of a Faculty is granted only if the person lectures or teaches reasonably regularly for that Faculty. A number of professional librarians are Faculty members.

 iii. Bodley's Librarian and the Officers (Keepers)—six of us—are automatically entitled to Fellowships. Other members of staff, because of their personal qualities, may be elected to a college Fellowship. Such elections are entirely at the discretion of the colleges.[21]

A fellow is a member of the collective teaching and administrative staff associated with a college. Most often a librarian is a fellow when a graduate degree in a subject field is held.

At the University of Bristol, the differentiation of librarians is not quite as developed as at Oxford. The most important aspect of the status of a librarian seems to be the type of library qualifications held.

Compensation. As is the case with librarians in the United States, the feeling at Oxford and Bristol among the librarians is that they do not receive salaries comparable to those of their teaching colleagues. This issue is exacerbated by the difference in appointment—twelve-months for librarians versus nine- or ten-months for teaching faculty. A commonality of spirit on this issue does come through from librarians in both countries.

Tenure. The concept of tenure is not applied in the same way in Britain as in the United States. At Oxford, the librarians are appointed for a probationary period, usually two years. Once this time has elapsed, they are "confirmed in post," equivalent to the U.S. understanding of tenure. If a librarian should be promoted to a new post, once again the librarian would be in a probationary period. This process is unlike the situation in the United States, where the award of tenure is granted to the individual and not to the position.[22]

A very similar practice is in effect at Bristol. Librarians are normally appointed at the academic-related rank on three years' probation. This probationary period is the same for the teaching faculty.[23]

Promotion. This is probably where the greatest difference exists between the practice in the United States and that in Britain. The standards as developed by ACRL call for the same (or analogous) ranks for the librarians as for the faculty. Therefore, a cataloger or reference librarian who is outstanding and meets the criteria for promotion could reach full rank in the position held. A designation of Assistant Librarian in either the Bodleian or at Bristol indicates a certain level of responsibility, and equates more closely with the position than with the expertise of the individual. There is no general provision for the librarian to be promoted within the position. This situation requires that a librarian who wishes more recognition or an increase in salary must move to a more senior position with different responsibilities or accept an administrative position. Often advancement is precluded by the lack of educational qualifications or training.

Leaves. At the Bodleian Library, the librarians are entitled to ask for "study leave" if there is a definite project they wish to undertake. There is no provision for the librarian to earn sabbatical time as there is in many institutions in the United States, and as provided for by the ACRL guidelines. Leave time at the Bodleian will be granted only if it is deemed beneficial. The amount of time taken can be no more than forty-two days in any two-year period.[24]

At Bristol, research leaves or sabbaticals are not normally available to librarians. However, special application for leave might be considered. The conditions and terms would vary greatly and would be considered exceptional.[25]

Research Funds. Apparently, it is not usual for librarians, or even faculty for that matter, to be granted funds in support of research by the university. It could be reasoned that, since promotion and tenure do not play as large a part in the career of the librarian as they do in the United States, support for projects that could aid in attaining tenure or promotion would not be as forthcoming.

At Oxford, only librarians who are members of one of the Faculties are likely to receive any financial support. The Bodleian, however, does have trust funds that can be used to support research.[26]

Higham states, "Research grant support would be exceptional."[27] Therefore, a major criterion by which faculty status is evaluated in the United States is almost totally missing in the United Kingdom. Evidently this situation is a direct result of the limited support for research by teaching faculty.

Academic Freedom. When the question was raised about whether librarians enjoyed the academic freedom that would allow them to pursue research or work interests without fear of jeopardy for their jobs because of an unpopular position or philosophy espoused, the usual reaction was one of personal support for the concept. There was no document at either university specifically mentioning this issue. Vaisey answered the question by stating, "Generally speaking, I think the answer is Yes."[28] Higham stated, "Since librarians are the servants of the University, the concept of academic freedom does not apply in precisely the same way. Librarians serve teachers and researchers and therefore only indirectly serve research and scholarship itself."[29]

CONCLUSIONS

Table 5.1 helps to clarify the findings on the status of librarians at the two universities considered in this study. It compares those results with the ACRL criteria and with the latest summation from the literature about the status of librarians in the United States.

Table 5.1

Comparative Status of ACRL criteria as applied to Oxford and Bristol universities

	ACRL CRITERIA	**USA**	**UK**	
			Oxford	*Bristol*
1.	Professional Responsibilities & Self-Determination	Yes	Yes	Yes
2.	Library Governance	Yes	Yes	Yes
3.	University Governance	Yes	Possibly	
4.	Compensation	No	No	No
5.	Tenure	Yes	Yes, with different criteria	
6.	Promotion	Yes	No	No
7.	Leaves	Yes	42 days	Exceptional
8.	Research Funds	Yes	No	No
9.	Academic Freedom	Yes	Yes, in principle	

Have university librarians in the United Kingdom achieved teaching faculty status? Have the United Kingdom librarians reached parity with their American counterparts? The answer as gained from the above study would be a qualified yes. On many of the points the privileges and responsibilities of the British librarians do not differ substantially from those of American librarians.

The ability of the librarians to determine their work responsibilities indicates they do have the right of self-determination. With the implementation of the proposed national standards for evaluating academic and academic-related staff, it is evident that librarians above the rank of assistant librarian are being considered on the same criteria as the teaching faculty.

Library governance in the two libraries studied does not seem to be very different from that which might be found in an American library. There are many ways for librarians to have a choice concerning the policies and procedures of the libraries. The two organizational structures illustrated above for Oxford and Bristol are not dissimilar from those found in many libraries in the United States, and would easily satisfy the expectations of this ACRL standard.

The ability of librarians to take part in the administrative council at Oxford University is dependent upon their level of qualifications, unlike the American situation where no distinction is made among librarians. The situation at Bristol is much more analogous to that in the United States.

On the point of compensation, it is rare among both U.S. and British librarians to feel that their remuneration is comparable to that of their teaching colleagues. If this were the only criterion on which librarians in either country were to be judged as to whether they had achieved faculty status, few if any librarians would be able to qualify.

Although tenure is not defined in exactly the same manner in the United Kingdom as it is in the United States, the principle remains. With the confirmation in post, a de facto tenure is achieved. So in both instances, a form of tenure is achieved and would be in the spirit of the ACRL standard.

Promotion, as usually practiced in American libraries, recognizes the individual for specific talents and abilities to do the job presently held. This is not the practice in the two British libraries studied here. Both libraries equated promotion with an advance in the hierarchical structure.

The questions of leaves and research funds are intricately entwined in most libraries. If a librarian is not eligible for a research leave or sabbatical, it is unlikely that research funds would be available. In the two university libraries studied here, it is uncommon for librarians to be granted either. Only in exceptional cases would leave or research support be given. The ACRL standards clearly call for leaves and research support to be granted to librarians with the same conditions as the teaching staff.

The final ACRL criterion discusses academic freedom. The concept of freedom of inquiry, which is called for in this standard, is felt to be met by the librarians involved in this study. Although there is not a formal tenure process, a relationship with the university does exist which assures some freedom in research. The lesser amount of research involvement expected of the librarians by the university could have an impact upon the relevance of this standard to the situations at these two libraries.

The faculty status of the librarians at Oxford University and the University of Bristol is not as well defined as stated in the ACRL standards. But, their status within the universities is understood and appears to be comparable to many librarians in the United States who have been granted faculty status. The historical differences between the two universities studied might suggest that a different relationship could exist between the librarians and their universities. Surprisingly, little tangible difference was discovered. The fact that both institutions are governmentally funded and administered would tend to cause them to be similar. The mandated external evaluations required by the government help to enforce uniform standards among the universities and reduce historical differences.

Although faculty status has been an issue among librarians in the United States for the last quarter century, it has been less discussed and debated within the United Kingdom. The literature, which is rampant with articles discussing the status of librarians within U.S. libraries, has less to say about the status of librarians in the United Kingdom. As we in the United States continue to struggle to resolve this issue to everyone's satisfaction, it will likely become a growing issue in the United Kingdom. In the years ahead, it will be interesting to monitor how this issue will develop for librarians. With new and increasing challenges facing librarians in the future, a more highly trained and specialized librarian will be needed. These challenges will require that the appropriate recognition be given to librarians for their role in the educational process of the university, both in the United States and in the United Kingdom.

NOTES

[1] "Membership Endorses Joint Resolution on Faculty," *College & Research Libraries News* 8 (September 1972):209-12.

[2] Emily Werrell and Laura Sullivan, "Faculty Status for Academic Librarians: A Review of the Literature," *College & Research Libraries* 48 (March 1987):95-103.

[3] Ibid., 96.

[4] Janet Krompart and Clara DiFelice, "A Review of Faculty Status Surveys, 1971-1984," *The Journal of Academic Librarianship* 13 (March 1987):14-18.

[5] Ibid., 15.

[6] Ibid., 16.

[7] Association of University Teachers, *The University Library* (London: Association of University Teachers, 1964), 6.

[8] Library Association, *Recommended Salaries and Conditions of Service for Non-University Academic Library Staff* (London: Library Association, 1978).

9A. Illes, "Ratcliffe in Camera," *Library Review* 31 (Summer 1982):85.

10David Vaisey, letter to author, November 25, 1987.

11Norman Higham, letter to author, December 18, 1987.

12Ibid.

13Vaisey, letter.

14Ibid.

15Ibid.

16Higham, letter.

17Vaisey, letter.

18Vaisey, letter.

19Higham, letter.

20Ibid.

21Vaisey, letter.

22Ibid.

23Higham, letter.

24Vaisey, letter.

25Higham, letter.

26Vaisey, letter.

27Higham, letter.

28Vaisey, letter.

29Higham, letter.

Part III
A HISTORICAL EXAMINATION OF ACADEMIC LIBRARIANSHIP

6

The College Library Section, 1889-1923
Predecessor to the Association of College and Research Libraries

Charles E. Hale

A PERSPICACIOUS BEGINNING: ACRL, 1889-1923

Academic librarians, since the inception of our profession, have played a significant role in its development. Six of the twenty-two librarians who affixed their signatures to the May 1853 call for a librarians' convention were college librarians. Chronological delimitations are necessarily somewhat arbitrary, but between the first librarians' convention of 1853 and the second, in 1876, the American system of collegiate education began to experience a transformation. Postsecondary educational institutions were to emerge from a chrysalid stage, characterized by a traditionally classical, elitist, textbook-recitation-centered methodology, and to undergo a radical metamorphosis. This premise is further supported by Nathaniel Stewart's bibliographical essay on the study of American college library history. In it, Stewart hypothesized:

> For a real understanding of the history of college libraries in this country one must contend with a tradition, long entrenched in the library profession, that the year 1876 marks the *genesis* of American librarianship. I prefer the position that 1876 represents a *renaissance* in American librarianship from a sort of chrysalis existence. College librarianship offers striking testimony in support of this position.[1]

If one carefully studies library literature during the period 1800-1876, it does reflect that forces were in operation during the last half of the nineteenth century which were to revolutionize the academic library and significantly alter the role of its librarian.

An "associational consciousness" for college librarians as a separate and distinct group from that of the American Library Association (ALA) had still not risen on the national scene at the time of the 1876 convention. The first instance of such a consciousness seems to have surfaced, momentarily, on a regional, grassroots level as soon as the following year, however. In 1877 the Annual University Convocations of the Regents of the State of New York appointed a Committee on Cooperation in Indexing and Cataloging in College Libraries. The committee's report appeared in the August issue of *Library Journal* of that year and alludes to the rising consciousness of unique concerns among academic libraries:

> Your committee, in reporting upon the subject referred to them, would respectfully recommend that the libraries of this state unite with the [American] Library Association in devising and carrying out its schemes for cooperation among all the libraries of the country. ... If, however, the college libraries require any special adaptation of this movement to themselves—if they have any special wants to be met—their librarians should bestir themselves at once. At present the work is chiefly in the hands of the public libraries. In deference to the colleges, it is proposed that the next meeting of the Association be held during their usual vacation—about the first of September. If our needs or our experiences suggest any plan, or any modification of a plan, for mutual assistance, they should then be made known.[2]

The members of this committee apparently felt no such need for modification or special adaptation, since the literature is devoid of any such action, before the ALA convention of 1889.

Lucy Jane Maddox carefully scrutinized the concerns and interests not only of college and university librarians but of others engaged in the practice of librarianship during the decade following the 1876 convention. In her dissertation, "Trends and Issues in American Librarianship as Reflected in the Papers and Proceedings of the American Library Association, 1876-1885," Maddox provides the following scenario. Addressing what she calls "special topics," defined as "library problems which were not considered major issues but significant enough to rate a place in the programs of the association during its beginning years,"[3] Maddox suggests that a trend toward recognizing the college library as a "special type" was just beginning to emerge at the end of the period of her study. With the exception that the *Library Journal*, the association's official journal, saw fit to entitle its October 1877 issue "The College Number," because it contained articles specifically oriented to the college library, Maddox's observations appear accurate.

Brief as this retrospective look might be, it does set the stage and provide a perspective for the establishment of the College Library Section of ALA. "Thirteen years after the founding of the American Library Association, thirteen persons came together on May 10, 1889, at St. Louis, Missouri, to consider the advisability of organizing a section of college librarians. They came from seven states and from libraries ranging in size from 16,000 volumes (Denison University) to 380,000 volumes (Harvard).[4] At this meeting, they took it upon themselves to recommend the formation of the first section of the ALA, the College Library Section.[5] It was W.I. Fletcher, librarian of Amherst, who moved

> that it is the sentiment of this meeting that at the next conference of the Association, a College Library Section be organized.[6]

At the ALA White Mountains Conference in New Hampshire on September 12, 1890, the College Library Section was duly organized. At 4:00 p.m. on that September afternoon, fifteen librarians, representing some of the most prestigious libraries in the country, gathered. They selected W.I. Fletcher as the section's first chairman and G.T. Little, Bowdoin College librarian, as its secretary. Thus, the section's inception, this simple, called meeting, apparently signified "formal" organization. No nominating committee was appointed, no membership dues were established or required, nor were criteria for membership in the section formulated or defined. Not until 1897 was a committee named to provide any "continuity of effort for the Section."[7] Similarly, the section appears hardly to have obtruded itself into the consciousness of its parent body. The ALA did not acknowledge, recognize, or even welcome the establishment of its first section. The 1890 September issue of the *Library Journal* noted the following in a brief reference on its editorial page:

> We should not overlook the foundation of the College Section this year. ... The College Libraries have needs and interests differing in many ways as radically from the Free Public Libraries as have the State Libraries.[8]

No "official" mention of the Section is made by ALA until a decade later, when the 1900 *Minutes* of that body's council reported:

> The State Libraries Section and the College Reference Section were re-established by vote of Council; and a Catalog Section was established in response to the vote requesting such a section, passed at the Round Table meeting on Cataloging topics.[9]

At the earlier 1897 Association Conference in Philadelphia, W.I. Fletcher suggested two items for the section's consideration: (1) improving the section's name, and (2) establishing *continuous* organization. A Committee on Organization (comprising Willard Austin, Cornell's reference librarian; Olive Jones, librarian at Ohio State University; and Clement W. Andrews, John Crerar librarian), was appointed to report back on the two proposed items at the close of the section's meeting. This committee, upon completion of its charge, suggested that the section be renamed the College and Reference Library Work Section. Having received no formal sanction at this meeting, G.W. Harris, acting chair of the sectional meeting in 1898, simply used College and Reference Library Section, when referring to the organization's name at the latter meeting. The word *work* never appeared in the section's name again.

Pertaining to Fletcher's second recommendation relating to "organizational continuity," the Committee on Organization had suggested

> that full privilege of taking part in the discussions of the Section be accorded to any member of the Association, who feels his work comes in this division, and further, ... that a committee of three be appointed with the responsibility of providing a suitable program for the next conference.[10]

Here again, the committee's recommendations fell short of their intended purpose. No mention was made of sectional officers or how they would be selected. No constitution or bylaws committee was established, nor would one be formed for another twenty-five years.

As college and university librarians faced the twentieth century, they were, as a section of ALA, to enter what I have chosen to describe as a period of sequestered professional internalization. The first two decades — specifically, 1900-1923 — are devoid, for the most part, of any substantial interactions with ALA. This period was marked by attention to matters such as the following:

1. Redefining, organizationally, the section's membership and structure

2. Attempting to resolve emerging differences between specialized interest groups within the sectional membership (i.e., reference librarians — particularly those representing public libraries — and academic librarians)

3. Attending to functions, activities, and publications of concern to its specialized interest groups

4. Attempting, in general, to respond to the increasing need for a common basis of standardized skills and adequate preparation of members in order to meet these needs

Each of these areas will be discussed briefly, since each impacted on the section's development and its maturation as a professional association.

MEMBERSHIP AND ORGANIZATIONAL CONCERNS

At the 1906 sectional meeting, C. Alex Nelson recommended the following resolution relevant to sectional membership: " ... that the Section should include all librarians of [educational institutions] and all persons [interested in reference work]."[11] To understand fully the significance of Nelson's resolution, which was to alter, at least in specificity, the College and Reference Library Section's membership, we need to look at the historical meaning of sectional membership. Here, it is necessary to speak briefly of the variations in meaning that existed before this 1906 resolution.

ALA's original constitution (1877) contained no article or reference to "sections" per se. The constitution simply stated: "Any person engaged in library administration may become a member of the Association by signing the Constitution and paying the annual assessment.[12] Meeting ALA membership requirements at that time meant, concurrently and automatically, meeting any sectional requirements. From the time the College Library Section emerged in 1889-1890, no sectional membership requirements existed. ALA membership automatically signified the right of any member to be a part of any sectional subgroup that might emerge. An 1893 revision of ALA's constitution made no alterations to the 1877 version of membership eligibility.

It was not until constitutional revisions in 1909, and again in 1921, that ALA made changes to sectional membership definitions. The bylaws to the 1909 constitution (Section 8a) read: "A member of the Association eligible under the rules of the section may become a member thereof by registering his or her name with the Secretary of the Section."[13] Section 10 of the same 1909 constitution continued: "Sessions of sections shall be open to any member of the Association, but no person may vote in any section unless registered as a member of the same."[14] It was not until the 1921 revision that ALA permitted sections to define their own membership. Section 12 of the bylaws to the ALA constitution of 1921 read:

> Sections, may, if they so select, charge annual dues, limit their own membership, issue publications, and in general carry on activities along the line of their own interest, accounting for their own funds solely to their own numbers.[15]

This brief synopsis of ALA's constitutional changes shows that Nelson's 1906 attempt to limit sectional membership preceded by fifteen years ALA's willingness to allow sections this prerogative. Although Nelson's recommendation in no way violated existing constitutional terminology, it was a definite sectional attempt to define more specifically those individuals, libraries, and interests to which the section would direct its attention and energies.

The College Library Section had, since its inception, been primarily an informal gathering of college and reference librarians having similar needs and interests. It was this characteristic which had prompted W.I. Fletcher to speak of the section's need for "organizational continuity" at its 1897 conference meeting. In his address to the membership, Fletcher stated:

> Simplicity is rightly regarded as the chief merit in such matters of organization, and it would seem quite sufficient that we would each year choose a chairman and a secretary for the Section. ... Their chief duty would be the arrangement, in consultation with the Executive Board of the Association, of the program for the Section's meetings.[16]

Fletcher's suggestions were adopted, and a committee was appointed to provide a suitable program for the next conference.

It was not until six years later, at the Niagara Falls Conference of 1903, that the section attended to Fletcher's first point—the manner of selecting section officers—by selecting a nominating committee. But this committee, responsible for proposing the section's chairman and secretary, would exist for only ten years, for in 1912 the section underwent further organizational change. Meeting in Ottawa, Canada that year, the nominating committee recommended a change in the ALA bylaws, which the association adopted, relative to the selection of a Committee on Arrangements.[17] Instead of electing a chairman and secretary to administer the section's affairs, the section would now elect a Committee on Arrangements consisting of three members. Later referred to as its Executive Committee or Committee on Management, this committee ran the section's business for another decade, until the College and Reference Library Section developed its own first bylaws in 1923.

A further reference to the informal nature of the section was made in 1920 by William Warner Bishop, librarian of the University of Michigan. For the first time in its history, ALA met in special session at Chicago, on June 1, 1920. Reflecting on the association's history at this session, Bishop commented on the ALA's provisions for sections:

> The present provisions for sections, I think you will find, is a loose one. It merely provides, practically, that they may exist—and we all know that some of the sections have been carefully organized and some very loosely organized. Those which have had the longest history and perhaps have performed the most valuable service to the Association, have been the most loosely organized of the lot. I refer, for example, to the Catalog Section and the College and Reference Section, neither of which has had specific organization and both of which have had programs which we have attended with great profit.[18]

REFERENCE LIBRARIANS AND REORGANIZATION

When in 1897 the Committee on Organization suggested that the name of the section be changed to College and Reference Library Work Section, it signalled an issue that was to arise often throughout the organization's history. In 1906 a motion to appoint a section committee of three to consider "the advisability of a more definite organization of college librarians ... and the desirability of separate organizations for college and reference librarians"[19] was passed by a vote of the membership, thirty-three to eighteen. However, the committee appointed to consider this question, when reporting back to the section stated, "In the opinion of the committee, the forming of such an organization was inexpedient."[20] This decision apparently stood until 1913, when discussion sessions of the section were divided between a College Librarians' Roundtable and a Reference Librarians' Roundtable. The following year, the officers of the section were authorized to "investigate as to the advisability of holding separate meetings for college librarians, apart from those of reference librarians."[21] After some discussion concerning appropriate officers and form of organization, "it was the sense of the meeting that the present form was satisfactory."[22] Again, the attempt at separation had failed.

These early attempts to postpone the splintering process within the section were only temporarily successful. Discontent and the inability of the organization to address itself to specialized needs were to plague the section throughout its history. Subsequently, however, as the section experienced similar discontent with its parent association, it tended to become increasingly amenable to accommodating the interests and needs of subgroups within the section's organizational family.

SECTIONAL PROGRAMS AND SELECTED ACTIVITIES, 1889-1923

Subjects of sectional programs and discussions at annual ALA conferences during the period 1889-1923 dealt with library techniques, bibliographical control, college and university statistics, library cooperation, and services to library users. A careful analysis of sectional programs during the period is summarized below. The topics are presented in descending order of frequency of their appearance during the period.[23]

Topic	Number of Times
Reference Work: Public Libraries	17
Cataloging/Classification	12
Seminary/Departmental Collections	9
Cooperative Efforts	9
Union Lists	8
Relation of College Library to Users	8
European Book Markets and the War	8
Introduction in Use of the Library	7
Library Buildings/Architecture	6
Interlibrary Loan	6
Teaching Bibliography to Students	6
Individual Library Descriptions	6
Collection Development	6

Although the list does not name each topic covered, it does reflect membership needs and interests. The replication of a number of the discussion topics and the frequency of their appearance are easily explained by the varying geographical locations of ALA conferences during the period. One might conclude as well that this geographical variance in no small way contributed to the lack of continuity in the College and Reference Library Section of which W.I. Fletcher spoke earlier.

The emergence of regional associations of college and university librarians may have been similarly fostered by geographic considerations, lack of travel funds, and the slow membership growth of the section at the national level. Regional associations appeared as early as 1907. The New England College Librarians' Association emerged in that year, the University and College Librarians of the Mid-West in 1910, and the Eastern College Librarians in 1912. These regional associations appear to have positively served as proving grounds for future ALA and sectional leaders. Similarly, there appears to be a definite correlation between topics discussed at regional association meetings and topics covered in the sectional programs at ALA annual conferences.

As mentioned earlier, additional activities of the section during this period were primarily introspective in nature. Energies were directed toward improving organizational structure and providing a national forum for resolution of problems of the constituencies represented. This process of organizational development progressed through increased use of committees. Nominating committees, committees on organization, and a committee on arrangements and programs emerged early in this period. Toward the end of the period, however, committees charged with specific tasks began to appear, such as:

- Committee on a Union List of Serials
- Committee on Educational Qualifications and Status of Professional Librarians in Colleges & Universities
- Committee on Regional Groupings of Libraries
- Committee on Standardization of Building Needs
- Committee on a Revised Form of Library Statistics
- Committee on Printed Cards for Monographic Series
- Committee on Foreign Periodicals of the War Period

Other activities, although not originally sponsored by or developed under sectional auspices, included the compilation of college and university statistics, the conduct of library surveys, and such cooperative ventures as union lists, indexes, and collection development guidelines.

The compilation of college and university library statistics, like that for public libraries, did receive impetus from the federal government, specifically, the U.S. Bureau of Education. One excellent example of such impetus in this area was the monumental 1876 compendium *Public Libraries in the United States*. This afforded to college and university librarians their most comprehensive statistical view up to that time of the libraries in their charge. Later, the bureau publications of 1893, 1895, 1896, 1897, and 1903 provided updates for the 1876 work.

In 1906 the College and Reference Library Section membership heard James Thayer Gerould, librarian of the University of Minnesota, present a paper entitled "A Plan for the Compilation of Comparative University and College Library Statistics."[24] Responding to a recommendation by Gerould, a committee was appointed to address the advisability of acquiring such information. After querying 100 selected college and university librarians, the committee rendered a report in 1907 recommending that similar compilations be made again the following year.

Gerould himself, while librarian at Minnesota, initiated the distribution of an annual sheet giving statistics for a select group of libraries. He continued the practice after his move to Princeton University in 1920, and his "Princeton Statistics" not only served as a valuable source of such information for several college and university librarians but ultimately became the basis for the Association of Research Libraries (ARL) statistics. Supplementing Gerould's list, ALA assumed responsibility for gathering statistics for both public and college libraries in the first quarter of the twentieth century.

During this same period, considerable activity and discussions were directed to interlibrary cooperation. Basil Stuart-Stubbs has traced the involvement of librarians, both public and college, in the development of cooperative ventures during the period 1889-1923. In his article,[25] he addressed the contributions of such college librarians as Joseph C. Rowell, Ernest C. Richardson, Charles H. Gould, and William C. Lane. That the College and Reference Library Section was involved in cooperative ventures, Stuart-Stubbs leaves little doubt. Although his study covered the subject only to the year 1910, it is a matter of record that the College and Reference Library Section continued to direct its attention toward cooperation. The sectional meetings in 1911, 1912, 1922, and its entire session in 1926, for example, included discussions on cooperative ventures.

College and university librarians were very much concerned during this period with the identification, location, and distribution of union lists and indexes. As early as 1893, Clement W. Andrews, the librarian of John Crerar Library in Chicago, spoke to the need for a checklist of scientific periodicals. Again, in 1901, in a communication read before the ALA council and executive board, Andrews's name appeared as one of a committee of three calling for an annual catalog of doctoral dissertations. In 1917 Andrews spoke to the College and Reference Library Section on a "Plan for a Census of Library Resources," describing his attempts to identify special library collections in the Chicago area.

Ernest C. Richardson, librarian at Princeton, concurred with Andrews in 1893 on the need for a checklist of scientific periodicals and moved for the adoption of the following resolution: " ... that all efforts toward checklists of the less common periodicals in our American libraries should have the heartiest cooperation of the college librarians."[26] Again in 1917, Richardson spoke before the section on the subject "The Return of Cooperative Indexing." Other topics of a similar nature, but not attributable to Richardson alone, reflected the section's concern for cooperative activities during this period. These included:

- a short story index (1912 meeting)
- the idea of a universal catalog (1919 meeting)
- a checklist of U.S. documents (1921 meeting)
- the eventual appearance of the *Union List of Serials* (in 1928), a project to which forty libraries, chiefly college and university, had contributed $12,000 a year for three years previously for its support and for which a sectional committee had existed.

Indeed, the period 1889-1923 appeared bleak in the area of ALA publishing and publications directed at college and university librarians. Andrew Keogh, librarian of Yale University, wrote in a 1902 article entitled "A.L.A. Publications for College and University Libraries":

> The A.L.A. is predominantly a public library organization. Its history, its membership, the papers read at its meetings, leave no doubt on this point. The existence of the College and Reference Section shows that scholarly things are not the Association's main concern. ... It is therefore proper that in the publications of our Association the emphasis should be laid on helps to readers in popular libraries.[27]

There is substantial evidence available that this public library emphasis of which Keogh spoke did in fact dominate the association's publications during this period. Perhaps also, as he suggested, this emphasis was indeed right and proper. Table 6.1, taken from Carolyn Foreman's "An Analysis of Publications Issued by the American Library Association, 1907-1957," supports Keogh's perception.[28]

David Kaser, professor at the Graduate Library School of Indiana University, noted also an absence of books and papers published before the turn of the century that dealt with academic libraries.[29] Kaser identified only one title, Hugh Williams's *College Libraries in the United States; Contributions toward a Bibliography* (Albany, N.Y.: University of the State of New York Press, 1899), which bibliographically addressed the subject of academic librarianship. Published as number 19 of the New York State Library's "Bibliographic Bulletin" series, it was the first attempt, Kaser concludes, to publicly "bibliographize" academic librarianship. Dorothy Alice Plum's *Bibliography of American College Library Administration, 1899-1926* (Albany, N.Y.: University of the State of New York Press, 1926), reveals the same condition observed by Kaser in the earlier period, that is "practically no books had been written ... no research investigations or empirical analyses reported."[30]

Perhaps the most useful overview of academic librarianship, and one that may have served as an impetus for the section's publication efforts in the second quarter of the century, was "College and Library News." This summary of literature relating to college and university libraries was initially prepared by

Table 6.1

ALA publications intended for librarians and lay library workers

INTENDED AUDIENCE	NUMBER OF ALA PUBLICATIONS	
	1907-1916	1917-1926
Librarians in:		
PUBLIC libraries	17	18
SCHOOL libraries	5	8
STATE LIBRARY agencies	3	5
COLLEGE or UNIVERSITY libraries	0	1
SPECIAL libraries	2	2
TWO or MORE TYPES of libraries	25	25
LAY LIBRARY workers	36	23
TOTALS	88	82

students of the New York Public Library School for the Eastern College Librarians' conferences. Following its first appearance, on November 27, 1920 in *Library Journal*, and covering the literature of academic librarianship from 1917-1920, this series was to undergo variations in later years in compiler, frequency, and medium of publication. The next twenty-five years of the section's history proved far more productive.

THE SECTION'S FIRST CONSTITUTION: 1923

Ninety librarians were present when the College and Reference Library Section met on Wednesday, April 25, 1923 in the Baptist church in Hot Springs, Arkansas.[31] No previous mention had been made of a Constitutional Committee report, nor did such notice appear in the advance program, as published in ALA's tentative program schedule. At the Hot Springs meeting it was F.L.D. Goodrich, associate librarian of the University of Michigan, who presented the report "Proposed By-Laws of the College and Reference Section of A.L.A." The preparation of this document had been entrusted to the work of three men: George B. Utley (librarian of the Newberry Library), Andrew Keogh, and William Warner Bishop. To appreciate fully the circumstances surrounding the document's preparation, content, and adoption, one must recognize the professional stature of these men and the respect they commanded. Each had held membership in ALA for more than twenty years. Each had held, or was to hold, the association's highest office, that of ALA president, within a decade of one another: Bishop in 1918-1919, Utley in 1922-1923, and Keogh in 1929-1930. One might assume therefore that the section's new bylaws would reflect close ALA affiliation, and so they did. One might also assume that because of their distinguished service, their active participation in sectional programs, and past leadership roles in the section, they required little time for the preparation of the bylaws and received little criticism regarding their contents.

These newly proposed bylaws resulted in the following changes in the section's organizational structure:[32]

1. The officers of the section were expanded from the chairman and a secretary to an additional position, that of treasurer. (The close ALA affiliation alluded to earlier is substantiated when one notes that the "Treasurer of the Section was the Treasurer of the A.L.A.")

2. An annual dues assessment of fifty cents was called for, payable to the treasurer in January of each year.

3. Duplicating, for all practical purposes, the Committee on Arrangements that existed previously, three "directors" were to be elected with terms of three years. These three directors with the chairman and secretary would constitute a "Board of Management." This board was responsible for the conduct of business between annual meetings. Both officers and directors were eligible for reelection.

4. Although no article in the bylaws dealt specifically with the section's name, it appears that with these new bylaws, the section's official name was shortened to "College and Reference Section" from the previous "College and Reference Library Section."

This first constitution then sets the stage for the next phase in the development of the organization. In just one year, these bylaws would undergo alteration. The segment that designated the ALA treasurer as treasurer of the section would be eliminated, and the treasury function would be assigned to the secretary of the section, that is, the secretary/treasurer. In view of the limited funds at the section's disposal, a bylaws requirement concerning an audit of the section's books was also eliminated.

SUMMARY

In the January 1945 issue of *Library Quarterly*, the noted library historian Jesse Shera wrote:

> At the turn of the [twentieth] century and after, American librarianship entered its professional adolescence. Extremely conscious of its own youth, awkwardness, and rapid growth, it was, nevertheless, quite proud of its approaching maturity—proud too, to have cast aside the remnants of its infancy.[33]

Although Shera was speaking of American librarianship in general, his statement could equally well be applied specifically to college and university librarianship. This professional adolescence, in relation to sectional development, could be characterized by the following stages.

1. Academic librarians, during the period 1876-1900, became aware of the fact that the purposes and direction of the parent association (ALA) were oriented both philosophically and pragmatically toward public libraries.

2. College, university, and reference librarians came together to form the first section of ALA, the College Library Section, in 1889, to resolve what they considered to be "specialized" library interests and concerns.

3. Developing a self-awareness and consciousness during the last quarter of the nineteenth century, the section worked to define its constituencies and the related specialized needs of those constituencies.

4. Attempting to adapt to the rapidly changing educational environment of which they were a part, these librarians passed through a period of "sequestered professional internalization," which was required to cope with changes that were taking place in the academic world. This period was characterized, first, by attention to techniques, publications, and standardization of skills, and, finally, by educational advancement.

5. Organized originally as an informal, rather elite, nonrepresentative segment of college, university, and reference librarians, the section acquired in 1923 a more formal structure than had previously existed. With the adoption of these bylaws, the sectional leadership encouraged membership expansion more representative of the diverse population eligible for inclusion in the organization.

Initially, the section displayed qualities closely akin to those that one would ascribe to a closed fraternal society. Early participants tended to come from institutions noted for their prestige and strong resources, rather than from the "have not" institutions. Rank-and-file participation was made difficult by geographical and economic considerations. Library administrators, rather than library assistants, almost exclusively attended sectional meetings. That the early participants in sectional meetings represented the more prestigious libraries and not general library interests is evident. Fifty-three percent of those libraries represented at the section's organizational meeting in 1890, some forty years later, were to become charter members of the ARL. That it was also nonrepresentative of the college and university librarians in general is evinced by the fact that section membership in 1936, almost a half-century after its formation, had still not reached 100 members.

Although extremely conscious of their youth, awkwardness, and development as a group, academic librarians were indeed proud of their newly established self-identity. Several library historians have suggested that academic librarians collectively did not possess or exhibit a sense of self-awareness or consciousness until the turn of the twentieth century. This study has documented that, as early as 1877, independent spirit had emerged on the part of a group of academic librarians in New York state. The commonality of purpose among librarians to which library historians alluded did exist, but a collective self-awareness was also taking root. In 1896, and again in 1897, college libraries were to address themselves to their specialized interests and display an identity separate and distinct from those of public librarians.

As the twentieth century began, the College and Reference Library Section entered a period of sequestered professional internalization. Energies and efforts were largely introspective in nature. This period of internalization, as evidenced by a review of the section's conference programs and discussions, was marked by attention to such matters as the following:

1. Redefining sectional membership and organizational structure

2. Addressing emerging differences among specialized interest groups within the section (i.e., reference librarians, particularly those representing public libraries, and college and university librarians)

3. Sponsoring functions, activities, and publications of interest to the specialized groups represented

4. Attempting, in general, to respond to the increasing need for a common basis of standardized skills and adequate preparation of members in order to meet environmental demands

Still maintaining a close association with ALA during this period, the section continue to struggle with membership issues, structural organization, and defining its place in the entire library associational community. After existing for almost thirty-four years as a loosely organized, informal gathering of college, university, and reference librarians, the section was finally to achieve professional maturity. The appearance of the section's first constitution in 1923 was to bring this chapter of "sequestered internalization" to an end. The College and Reference Library Section in its new quarter century would play a significant role in the development of ALA and in the profession of librarianship.

NOTES

[1] Nathaniel Stewart, "Sources for the Study of American Library History, 1800-1876," *Library Quarterly* 13 (July 1943):227.

[2] "Co-operative College Cataloging," *Library Journal* 1 (August 31, 1877):435-36.

[3] Lucy Jane Maddox, "Trends and Issues in American Librarianship as Reflected in the Papers and Proceedings of the American Library Association, 1876-1885" (Ph.D. diss., University of Michigan, 1958), 496.

[4] U.S. Bureau of Education, *Report of the Commissioner of Education for the Year, 1889-1890*, vol. 2, pt. 2 (Washington, D.C.: Government Printing Office, 1893):1600-1609.

[5] Although the Publishing Section was formed in 1886, and a State Libraries Section in 1889, the former represented an ALA effort to systematize the association's publishing activities and was not representative of any specific group of specialized libraries within ALA. The latter section was organized as an "affiliated" section, rather than as an ALA sectional subdivision.

[6] "A.L.A. College Library Section," *Library Journal* 14 (May-June 1889):295.

[7] "The College Section of the A.L.A.," *Library Journal* 22 (October 1897):160.

[8] "Editorial," *Library Journal* 15 (September 1890):259.

[9] "Transactions of Council and Executive Board," *Library Journal* 19 (December 1896):154.

[10] "College and Reference Section," *Library Journal* 23 (August 1898):172.

[11] "College and Reference Section," *Library Journal* 31 (June 1906):233.

[12] "American Library Association," *Library Journal* 1 (March 31, 1877):253.

[13] "Handbook, 1910," *ALA Bulletin* 15 (September 1921):268.

[14] Ibid.

[15] "A.L.A. Handbook, 1921," *ALA Bulletin* 15 (September 1921):268.

[16] "The College Section of the A.L.A.," *Library Journal* 22 (October 1897):159.

[17]"College and Reference Section," *ALA Bulletin* 6 (January 1912):294.

[18]"Revision of Constitution," *ALA Bulletin* 14 (January 1920):13.

[19]"College and Reference Section," *Library Journal* 31 (June 1906):233.

[20]Ibid.

[21]"College and Reference Section," *Library Journal* 39 (July 1914):549.

[22]Ibid.

[23]The information in this table is based on an analysis of "College Library Section and College and Reference Library Sections" found in *Library Journal* and the *ALA Bulletin* for time period covered.

[24]James T. Gerould, "A Plan for the Compilation of Comparative University and College Library Statistics," *Library Journal* 31 (November 1906):761-63.

[25]Basil Stuart-Stubbs, "An Historical Look at Resource Sharing," *Library Trends* 23 (April 1975):649-66.

[26]"College Library Section," *Library Journal* 18 (September 1893):91.

[27]Andrew Keogh, "A.L.A. Publications for College and University Libraries," *ALA Bulletin* 16 (July 1922):106.

[28]Carolyn Foreman, "An Analysis of Publications Issued by the American Library Association, 1907-1957" (Master's thesis, University of Texas, 1959), 69.

[29]David Kaser, "A Century of Academic Librarianship as Reflected in the Literature," *College & Research Libraries* 37 (March 1976):110-27.

[30]Ibid.

[31]"College and Reference Section," *ALA Bulletin* 17 (July 1923):277.

[32]"By-Laws of the College and Reference Section of the American Library Association," ALA College and Reference Section Correspondence, 1931, (Series 35/1/15) Box 5, ALA Archives, University of Illinois, Urbana.

[33]Jesse H. Shera, "The Literature of American Library History," *Library Quarterly* 15 (January 1945):15.

7

An Uncertain Crusade
The History of Library Use Instruction
In a Changing Educational Environment

Larry Hardesty and John Mark Tucker

JUSTIN WINSOR AND THE EARLY YEARS: 1880-1900

In 1880, during his third year as Harvard University librarian, Justin Winsor examined the contemporary collegiate environment. Observing a new interest in academic "libraries as educational agencies," he proclaimed that the college library had embarked on a "new career."[1] Winsor's stature in the profession of librarianship demands that the historical significance of this assertion not be overlooked. An examination of Winsor's comment, in the context of his times, necessarily raises a question about the extent to which academic libraries truly began a new era. The corollaries to this question are twofold: what were the academic library's educational purposes, and what were its functions in the new career?

This contribution addresses these questions and provides an overview of library use instruction as it related to the broader, higher educational environment over the past century. At times, students, professors, administrators, and other contemporaries simply dismissed it as irrelevant to the educational enterprise. Nevertheless, despite the varying degrees of success or failure that library use instruction experienced during any particular period, it may be considered as symbolic of (1) the academic library's attempt to respond to fluctuating demands for information, services, and collections, and (2) the efforts of academic librarians to earn a permanent and respected niche in the higher education establishment. At times, library use instruction lagged behind the national climate of higher education while, at other times, it anticipated the future.

Returning briefly to Winsor himself, it is notable that his achievements included being director of the library at what many regarded as the nation's leading academic institution, Harvard University. His professional stature, however, is based on reasons other than his Harvard connections. He assisted in the founding of the *Library Journal* and of the American Library Association (ALA), of which he served as president from 1876 to 1885. He headed the American delegation to both the first International Conference of Librarians in 1877 and the second international conference twenty years later.

Winsor's four-volume *Memorial History of Boston* (1880-1881) and his eight-volume *Narrative and Critical History of America* (1886-1889) earned wide acclaim and established his reputation as a historian and a cartographer. Beginning in 1886, he served a term as president of the American Historical Association. Collectively, these accomplishments mark him as a scholar-librarian, a kind of intellectual and administrative prototype for academic librarianship in the latter part of the nineteenth century.

The context for Winsor's statement about the "new career," and his belief that by 1880 academic libraries had entered a new age, must be reviewed against the backdrop of higher education at mid-century. Despite repeated calls for reform, higher learning in 1865 remained much as it had been decades earlier. The old-time liberal colleges prevailed throughout the years leading up to and including the War Between the States. Through the traditional methods of memorization and recitation, these colleges fulfilled their purpose of training young men to meet their professional and civic obligations. Typically, the college president provided the capstone of the curriculum (which had drawn its strength from the *trivium* and *quadrivium* of the medieval university) through instruction in mental or moral philosophy. This course attempted to reconcile reason and the natural law (as defined by seventeenth and eighteenth century philosophers) with Christian theology. It featured the best efforts of a president to bring his intelligence, knowledge, and personality to bear on a student's world view.

Mark Hopkins, president of Williams College from 1836 to 1872, symbolized the old-time professor who described his task as touching the souls of men with the truth of moral wisdom. He once said to a colleague, "I don't read books, in fact I never did read any books."[2] Hopkins inspired an oft-repeated phrase first uttered by another famous American, James A. Garfield, that the "ideal college" was "Mark Hopkins on one end of a log and a student on the other."[3] By 1867 Ralph Waldo Emerson had written that a new era in collegiate education finally had arrived on the horizon—both recent and upcoming developments represented a "cleavage occurring in the hitherto granite of the past."[4] No longer would President Hopkins be alone on a log with a student; the two would be joined by books and libraries.

A combination of national and international forces brought about the demise of the old-time college as the prevailing mode in higher education. Consciously imitating their German counterparts, American professors, a number of whom had engaged in doctoral studies in Germany, began promoting research culminating in the Ph.D. degree. Moral and mental philosophy and political economy splintered into more specialized social science disciplines. Recently trained professors in these fields established new associations, conducted original research, and published their findings. History and other humanistic disciplines also adopted the research ideal and joined the social sciences in support of the notion of the library as a laboratory, a concept corresponding to the function of a laboratory in the physical sciences. The establishment of land-grant universities signaled the democratization of higher education, encompassed the experimental methods and laboratory tools of the scientist, and moved the university inexorably closer to the role of problem solver for industry and agriculture.

All these trends resulted in unprecedented growth in the production of knowledge as well as faculty and student demands for library resources and services. Between 1870 and 1890, the number of academic institutions grew from 563 to 998. From 1875 to 1891, libraries greatly increased their book collections: Pennsylvania and Columbia quadrupled their holdings from 25,000 to 100,000 and from 33,000 to 135,000 volumes, respectively. The size of Cornell's collection jumped more than tenfold, from 10,000 to 111,000 volumes. Accordingly, librarians became interested in making their collections more accessible. In 1876 the Columbia library opened only twelve hours per week; twenty years later that had increased to ninety-eight hours. Comparable data from Yale and Harvard demonstrate a change from thirty-six to seventy-two hours and from forty-eight to eighty-two hours, respectively.[5]

The new ideals of graduate research, disciplinary specialization, and scholarly production were accompanied by another development that had profound implications for how books and libraries would be used—the advent of seminar instruction. In 1886 Melvil Dewey wrote that "professor after professor sends his classes, or goes with them to the library and teaches them to investigate for themselves and to *use* books, getting beyond the method of the primary school with its parrot-like recitations from a single text."[6] A number of professors corroborated Dewey's observation, among them Johns Hopkins historian Herbert Baxter Adams, who, in addressing a librarian audience, recounted the work of several of his colleagues who conducted scientific historical research and used seminar teaching methods.[7] Samuel Rothstein described the "distinctive feature of the seminar" as the "first-hand investigation of original material by the students under the close supervision of the professor. Preferably this process would take place in the library itself."[8] Thus, as the century drew to a close, the vision of Mark Hopkins and the log diminished in relevance. Moreover, the librarians who, along with professors, had been caught up in the swirling change and growth that marked the age, continued to seek concepts for the academic library that would help them earn a place in the academic community. Amidst this unrest, Winsor proclaimed the library's new career: the instruction of students in use of the library.

Meanwhile, at Harvard, Winsor took the lead in opening up to his scholarly clientele the university's rich library resources. He enlarged the reserve book collection, authorized stack privileges for students, and brought a number of small libraries into the main building. He prepared a union list of serials holdings for libraries in the Boston-Cambridge area and encouraged interlibrary loans. Physical improvements included installation of electric lights, new furniture, and better ventilation. Winsor regarded instruction in library use as integral to his commitment to liberalize and expand the intellectual value of the college library, bringing it more fully into the teaching and learning process.[9] Nearly twenty years after Winsor's death, Ernest Cushing Richardson of Princeton would describe Winsor's appointment as "professor of books" and his work at Harvard as watershed events in the history of bibliographic instruction.[10]

Library use instruction emerged, then, as one key element in an array of library services, nurtured and promoted among members of the profession by one of the nation's leading academic librarians as essential to library efforts to respond to an increasingly complex and rapidly changing academic environment.

User instruction in the Winsor model, indeed, may have been merely one response to the changing circumstances, perhaps only equal in value to numerous others. Still, Winsor had embraced library use instruction as the symbol of the arrival of a new age.

Librarians across the nation joined Winsor in his enthusiasm for instructing library users and, collectively, they engaged in wide experimentation. The optional course in bibliography emerged as an important feature of user instruction during the last two decades of the nineteenth century. The course frequently emphasized descriptive bibliography and the history of books and libraries, but it typically contained a substantial library use component. Usually taught by the college librarian, it included instruction in enumerative bibliography, designed to show students how to determine the intellectual contents of books. It introduced undergraduates to indexes, bibliographies, and other reference sources of both a general and specialized nature. Other methods included book talks, bibliographic lectures, and orientation tours. The library community, however, did not produce any established structures or even generally accepted methods for effective instruction. The quality and style of approaches varied widely from institution to institution. Nevertheless, librarians did begin the dialogue about the nature and purposes of user instruction. They called for clearly stated objectives for their programs, attempted a variety of methods, and, of perhaps greatest importance, caught a vision of the library's educational potential.

BUREAUCRACY, EXPERIMENTATION, AND PHILANTHROPY 1901-1940

After the turn of the century, higher education solidified the gains it had made in the previous century. Arthur E. Bestor, Jr. described the period from 1875 to 1917 as a time of transformation in American scholarship; the ideals of research, technical training, and liberal education in all of their diversity became fully operative, achieving professional, intellectual, and bureaucratic stability.[11] The large land-grant universities grew in size and in intellectual stature, symbolizing new national attitudes about higher education as a whole. Regarded by many as more useful to society than the old-time liberal arts college, the burgeoning universities demanded of their own libraries a greater capacity to support research, service, and related institutional goals.

The libraries themselves emerged at once both more bureaucratic and more service-oriented. Librarians committed to user instruction took courage both from their rapidly expanding new collections and from a stronger service ethic. Vast and complicated library resources offered tacit testimony to the student's desperate need of assistance and instruction. Rothstein defined the period from 1896 to 1916 as the decades that marked the integration of reference services into the permanent administrative structure of research libraries.[12] The appointment of full-time reference librarians supplied a source of moral support for advocates of instruction. It should be noted, however, that while instruction in library use became as visible as reference work, it did not become as stable. Library use instruction failed in its attempts to obtain widespread or long-term curricular acceptance of credit courses, perhaps because the successful programs had depended so heavily on the personal and intellectual traits of the librarian-instructors. Individuals such as H. L. Koopman at Brown, Azariah Smith Root at Oberlin, George T. Little at Bowdoin, and Winsor at Harvard were too seldom succeeded by someone of equal classroom presence.[13] Likewise, user instruction failed in its efforts at full integration into the personnel, service, and bureaucratic structures of academic libraries, perhaps because of its inadequately developed conceptual and theoretical foundations.[14]

As if to quell their uncertainties, librarians conducted a number of surveys in their attempts to verify the supposed popularity of user instruction. William Austen's 1913 survey for the New York State Library Association found that 49 percent of the 165 respondents engaged in some type of instructional program, while an ALA survey conducted a year earlier found that 57 percent of 149 responding institutions offered required or elective courses. In 1914 Henry Evans reported that 20 percent of 446 colleges and universities and 56 percent of 166 normal schools provided instruction in library use.[15]

After World War I, higher education entered a new and discouraging phase. Grants from private foundations, while totaling in the hundreds of millions of dollars, fell considerably below earlier (but unrealistic) expectations. External funds could be expected to stimulate educational innovation and enhance permanent endowments, but benefactors did not intend that educators should regard the funds as essential to the annual budgetary process. Moreover, students seemed more obsessed than usual with noneducational matters. Laurence Veysey described the general mood of the academic community as lacking confidence and fearing economic scarcity. Educators in the 1920s and 1930s confronted a social pattern hostile in spirit to the entire curriculum.[16]

Yet amazingly, out of this era of discontent in higher education arose some of the most compelling curricular innovations of the twentieth century. Disciples of John Dewey urged instructional emphasis on family and social development and civic responsibility. Robert Hutchins and Alexander Meiklejohn attempted new philosophical constructs for the liberal arts. Honors courses were established, and Veysey concluded that by the end of the 1930s "there seemed far more likelihood of widespread curricular rethinking than at any time during the preceding thirty years.[17]

Simultaneously, academic libraries entered an equally fruitful phase, especially in the small liberal arts colleges that benefited from private philanthropy. In 1929 the Carnegie Corporation initiated its program of book collection support, distributing grants of $5,000 to $25,000 to eighty-one institutions, thereby stimulating numerous presidents and trustees to consider a more central role for the library in collegiate education. Carnegie eventually extended these grants to junior colleges and normal schools, as well as to black colleges and universities.[18]

The educational climate of this period proved most hospitable to user instruction, which advanced both conceptually and programmatically. In 1935 Louis Shores published his first full statement of the "library-college" idea, thus defining the teaching function of academic libraries and redirecting for several decades the continuing dialogue on the library's purpose. (Even today, library-college ideology holds considerable appeal because of its philosophical coherence, but its application has been neither practical nor widespread.) B. Lamar Johnson, as a college dean and library director, implemented course-related library use instruction throughout the curriculum at Stephens College. Harvie Branscomb conducted research based on library use and urged a stronger library-professor partnership. He published his results in *Teaching with Books*,[19] which remains a classic in the literature of librarianship. As a preview of things to come (some forty years later), the 1930s also ushered in the first substantial research, based on valid design and measurement techniques, that treated the topics of student knowledge and use of library resources. Studies by library science professor Peyton Hurt and psychologists C.M. Louttit and James Patrick are among the earliest examples.[20]

The educational environment of the entire period from 1901 to 1940 can be considered unusual—if not ironic. Early on, the inability of user instruction advocates to achieve broad curricular acceptance in the form of credit courses and their lack of success in gaining adequate support from within the library community greatly discouraged them. Yet during the 1930s, even with the depression and a general lack of self-confidence throughout higher education, instruction advocates furthered their cause substantially. Still, despite the achievement of new levels of sophistication both intellectually and programmatically, their experiences from the 1930s would leave them only marginally prepared for the unexpected changes that would accompany and follow World War II.

BRICKS, BOOKS, AND THE SEARCH FOR IDENTITY
1941-1968

The 1941-1968 period of library use instruction began much as the 1901-1940 period ended—with an attempt by an influential librarian to educate a nonlibrarian audience. The year after the publication of Harvie Branscomb's *Teaching with Books*, Louis Round Wilson, perhaps the most influential librarian of his day, made a presentation to the Institute for Administrative Officers of Higher Education entitled "The Use of the Library in Instruction."[21] Wilson confidently declared:

> I believe the efficiency of the library as an educational instrument can likewise be further increased, provided the problem is steadily and intelligently attacked by college administrators, faculties, librarians, and research students.[22]

Despite such an optimistic beginning, Barbara Phipps's investigation of librarians involved in user instruction in the late 1960s found them frustrated, disappointed, and demoralized because of "lack of staff, lack of time, lack of money for experimentation, lack of cooperation and interest from the faculty and the administration."[23] The evolution of library use instruction during the intervening years can best be understood in the framework of the growth of higher education during the same period.

Before World War II, only a small segment of the population attended college. By the late 1940s, however, a more meritocratic philosophy had combined with the GI Bill of 1944 to extend the opportunity for higher education to a deluge of returning veterans. The launching of Sputnik I by the Soviet Union in the next decade provided the impetus for a second major shift in American philosophy of higher education. Egalitarian ideals and support for national defense came to champion admission to colleges and universities for everyone.

With the swelling enrollments came increased funding. Nevertheless, academic libraries struggled to keep pace with the growth in higher education during this period. For example, in 1939-1940, academic libraries received less than $20 million and added only 3 million volumes to their collections. This expenditure, however, represented 3.7 percent of general and educational expenditures in higher education that year. This percentage dropped to 3.3 by 1950, and it did not regain the 3.7 figure until near the end of the "golden years" of the 1960s.[24]

Pivotal to understanding the development of library use instruction during this period is the fact that much of the increased funding for academic libraries went to "bricks and books." By 1967-1968, academic libraries annually added more than 22 million volumes to their collections.[25] The need for room, to house both growing collections and student populations, and for support by federal funds, resulted in a post-World War II library building spree that did not end until the 1970s. Meanwhile, the student-to-librarian ratio continued to increase. For example, from 1959 to 1969, the ratio of students to academic librarian increased from 378 to 446, or 23 percent.[26]

Activity without progress characterized library use instruction during this period. Numerous programs existed at the freshman orientation and basic instruction levels, but the increasing number of students overwhelmed many of even the well-established advanced efforts. As early as 1949, Erickson reported insufficient numbers of library personnel as the most serious deterrent to successful library instruction programs.[27] Faced with larger freshman classes each year and with little time to experiment and reflect, librarians of the day made little progress in offering effective library instruction. Thus, according to Brough, during this period library use instruction remained an "unsolved problem."[28]

Programs also struggled because they lacked a viable conceptual framework and because many librarians lacked a comprehension of either previous or concurrent efforts. Some librarians opposed user instruction from practical or philosophical viewpoints.[29] Kirk analyzed programs during the 1940s and 1950s and reached the following conclusions.

1. Those involved failed to distinguish orientation from instruction and therefore provided only the former.
2. The instruction or orientation was not given in a context of the student's need to know how to use the library.

3. The instruction that went beyond orientation tended to take its scope and content from the reference training that librarians had received.
4. Librarians were not sensitive to educational changes that were occurring.[30]

The same educational conditions that forced librarians to accommodate unprecedented growth in enrollments and collections after World War II also retarded the development of adequate user instruction. An unstated premise underlying Kirk's assessment is that librarians responded primarily to concerns of urgency rather than to concerns of more enduring significance.

Librarians turned to other solutions during the 1960s, such as the use of technology,[31] and the library-college movement. The latter, led by Louis Shores, attracted widespread attention in its efforts to change the entire structure of higher education.[32] In addition, during this time, Patricia Knapp planted the intellectual seeds resulting from the Monteith College project that would considerably influence later instructional efforts.[33] Nevertheless, the period ended, as Phipps found in 1968, with many librarians involved in user instruction frustrated and demoralized.[34]

A GRASSROOTS MOVEMENT AND GROWING SOPHISTICATION 1969-1980s

Ironically, library use instruction acquired momentum just as financial support and enrollments slowed dramatically. After a century of relatively steady and certain growth, American higher education in the late 1960s became "unsteady and uncertain."[35] This retrenchment started a ripple effect initially in academic libraries, which, in turn, affected library use instruction.

First, as Kaser described in his essay on "the revolution of 1969-1970," the change had a significant effect on the leadership of academic libraries caused by the "frustration of unrealized expectations."[36] For example, despite the biggest building boom in library history, book collections grew faster than the space to hold them, and overcrowding in libraries worsened.[37]

Second, potential scholars who in better economic times might have pursued careers in the classroom now entered academic librarianship. They brought with them an increased sophistication and added to an already awakening profession elements of "social responsibilities" that grew out of the 1960s. Perhaps remembering their own days as undergraduates during the high "baby boom" enrollments of the 1960s, these new librarians expressed a strong concern for undergraduate students. The leadership of Evan Farber, Miriam Dudley, and others of a previous generation notwithstanding, librarians in their twenties and thirties dominated the grassroots library use instruction movement of the early 1970s. Disenchanted with old solutions, these librarians looked to other methods to involve the academic library in the educational process.

To those unaware of the previous history of library use instruction, it would seem that it suddenly materialized in the late 1960s. With Farber's presentation in 1969 to the College Libraries Section of the Association of College and Research Libraries (ACRL) followed by Kennedy's article in *Library Journal*[38] the Earlham College program became widely known. By 1971 library use instruction had emerged as an authentic movement with its own annual conference at Eastern Michigan University and an ad hoc Committee on Bibliographic Instruction within the ACRL. Between 1969 and 1971, the intensity of experimentation in library use instruction greatly increased.[39]

By the mid-1970s the number of professional positions available for instructional librarians had grown significantly. (Previously, instructional reponsibilities had been merely tacked on to a general or specialized reference position, though some institutions created separate positions.) The number of articles on library use instruction indexed in *Library Literature* doubled from thirty-five in 1958 to seventy in 1971.[40] Articles by Farber,[41] Dillon[42] Frick,[43] and others offered more nuanced and sophisticated interpretations of user instruction than had been previously available. The newly formed Bibliographic Instruction Section would, by the end of the decade, become the most active section within the ACRL.

Just as the professoriate regrouped following student unrest in the mid-to-late 1960s and early 1970s, an economic recession began to dominate higher education. The capping of the number of tenured professorships available in a given department or even in an entire institution, coupled with other similar administrative responses to the recession, stimulated the growth of a large corps of "gypsy-scholars"—humanities and social science professors who moved from institution to institution, filling in for temporary vacancies and sabbatical leaves. Many of these underemployed professors moved into academic librarianship and added another important factor (through recent scholarship) to the accelerated development of library use instruction.

Part of the credit for the recently increased growth and maturity in library instruction programs also is owed to the Council on Library Resources, which through its philanthropic efforts supplied academic libraries with $3 million in grants over a period of nearly ten years. Further credit is owed to the guidance provided by individual advocates of library use instruction. By the late 1970s, librarians who had been involved in the early revival of user instruction (Evan Farber, Hannelore Rader, Carla Stoffle, and others) had moved into leadership positions both in professional associations and in academic libraries. In the late 1980s, library use instruction achieved a new level of maturity marked by the establishment of its own journal, *Research Strategies*, and the publication of several monographs and collected works.[44]

CONCLUSION

As the recent revival of library instruction strives for maturity and acceptance without loss of momentum, it is desirable to review the past—both distant and immediate. An examination of the records of the past century reveals that library use instruction has had an uneven and uncertain history. Even as recently as the late 1970s, Farber and Kirk, staunch advocates of library use instruction, admitted that "one looks almost in vain for serious recognition of bibliographic instruction by college and university faculty administrators."[45] While the Council on Library Resources provided a major impetus to the development of library instruction programs during the 1970s, Gwinn, in her review of the programs supported by the council, strongly questioned their success.[46] Other observers continue to criticize library use instruction for "lack of conceptual definition, spotty research, uneven financial support, and insufficient endorsement outside the library community."[47]

During the past hundred years, library use instruction clearly has been influenced by its surrounding environment of higher education. At times instructional programs have flourished because preeminent and farsighted individuals, such as Justin Winsor, have recognized changing currents in higher education and employed library use instruction to propel the academic library into a more intellectually useful direction. At other times, these programs have waned because of the inability of individuals to capitalize on the advances of their predecessors or because of the willingness of librarians during a given period merely to acquiesce to conditions rather than to anticipate and lead.

Surprisingly, the general availability of resources in higher education has not necessarily had a salutatory influence on user instruction. Both the 1930s and 1970s, times of economic scarcity in higher education, were characterized by innovation and progress in user instruction.[48] The relative prosperity of the 1920s, 1950s, and 1960s, however, brought little headway. Adversity may, indeed, engender innovation and creativity.

Given the history of its growth and development, library use instruction could be entering a "golden period." Advocates may have anticipated the renewed interest in undergraduate education of the 1980s, as evidenced by the recent publication of numerous books and reports on the subject.[49] Moreover, proponents of instruction currently occupy many of the leadership positions in academic libraries and professional library associations. In addition, the continuing adverse economic conditions of higher education may discourage the complacency of the more prosperous periods and encourage the innovation and creativity characteristic of user programs in the 1930s and 1970s.

Predictions of the future always involve uncertainty. It remains to be seen whether a revitalization of undergraduate education will in fact occur and, if it does occur, what functions the academic library and library use instruction will perform. Has the recent resurgence of library use instruction merely been part of a cyclical pattern? Will the enthusiasm for it wane as other concerns, such as those related to collection development, preservation of materials, computer technology, and periodical costs, capture the attention and consume the energies of more and more librarians? It could well be that, instead of a "golden period," the next phase of instruction in library use may be one of reduced expectations.

NOTES

[1] Justin Winsor, "College Libraries as Aids to Instruction: The College Library," in *Circulars of Information of the Bureau of Education* 1 (1880):14.

[2] Frederick Rudolph, *Mark Hopkins and the Log: Williams College, 1836-1872* (New Haven: Yale University Press, 1956), 77.

[3] Ibid., 225-31. See also, *Mark Hopkins' Log and Other Essays By Louis Shores*, ed. John David Marshall (Hamden, Conn.: Shoe String Press, 1965).

[4] Quoted in Walter P. Rogers, *Andrew D. White and the Modern University* (Ithaca, N.Y.: Cornell University Press, 1942), 4.

[5] See John Mark Tucker, "The Origins of Bibliographic Instruction in Academic Libraries, 1876-1914," in *New Horizons for Academic Libraries*, ed. R.D. Stueart and R.D. Johnson (New York: K.G. Saur, 1979), 268-76. See also Frederick Rudolph, *The American College and University: A History* (New York: Vintage, 1962); Jurgen Herbst, *The German Historical School in American Scholarship: A Study in the Transfer of Culture* (Ithaca, N.Y.: Cornell University Press, 1965); Laurence R. Veysey, *The Emergence of the American University* (Chicago: University of Chicago Press, 1965); and Orvin Lee Shiflett, *The Origins of American Academic Librarianship* (Norwood, N.J.: Ablex, 1981).

[6] Melvil Dewey, "Libraries the True University for Scholars as Well as People," *Library Notes* 1 (1886):49-50.

[7] Herbert Baxter Adams, "Seminary Libraries and University Extension," *Johns Hopkins University Studies in Historical and Political Science* 5 (1887):443-59.

[8] Samuel Rothstein, *The Development of Reference Services through Academic Traditions, Public Library Practice and Special Librarianship* (Chicago: Association of College and Reference Libraries, 1955), 12.

[9] Wayne Cutler and Michael H. Harris, "Winsor, Justin (1831-1897)," *Dictionary of American Library Biography* (Littleton, Colo.: Libraries Unlimited, 1978), 570-72; Robert E. Brundin, "Justin Winsor of Harvard and the Liberalizing of the College Library," *Journal of Library History* 10 (1975):57-70.

[10] Ernest C. Richardson, "Extracts from a Paper on the Place of the Library in a University," in *American Library Institute Papers and Proceedings*, ed. A.S. Root (Chicago: American Library Association, 1916), 169-81.

[11]Arthur E. Bestor, Jr., "The Transformation of American Scholarship, 1875-1917," *Library Quarterly* 23 (1953):164-79.

[12]Rothstein, *The Development of Reference Services*, 34-36.

[13]Peter Hernon, "Instruction in the Use of Academic Libraries: A Preliminary Study of the Early Years as Based on Selective Extant Manuscripts," *Journal of Library History* 17 (1982):16-38.

[14]John Mark Tucker, "Emerson's Library Legacy: Concepts of Bibliographic Instruction," in *Increasing the Teaching Role of Academic Libraries*, ed. Thomas G. Kirk (San Francisco: Jossey-Bass, 1984), 15-24; Edward G. Holley, "Academic Libraries in 1876," *College & Research Libraries* 37 (1976):43.

[15]Mary E. Ahern, "Library Activity During 1912-13," in *Report of the Commissioner of Education for the Year Ended June 30, 1913* (Washington, D.C.: Government Printing Office, 1914), vol. 1, p. 327; John D. Wolcott, "Recent Aspects of Library Development," in *Report of the Commissioner of Education for the Year Ended June 30, 1912* (Washington, D.C.: Government Printing Office, 1913), vol. 1, pp. 381-82; Henry R. Evans, comp. "Library Instruction in Universities, Colleges, and Normal Schools," *U.S. Bureau of Education Bulletin* 34 (1914):3.

[16]Laurence R. Veysey, "Stability and Experimentation in the American Undergraduate Curriculum," in *Content and Context: Essays on College Education*, ed. Carl Kaysen (New York: McGraw-Hill, 1973):1-63.

[17]Ibid., 10.

[18]Wilhelm Munthe, *American Librarianship from a European Angle* (Chicago: American Library Association, 1939), 99-100; Neil A. Radford, *The Carnegie Corporation and the Development of American College Libraries, 1928-1941* (Chicago: American Library Association, 1984).

[19]Harvie Branscomb, *Teaching with Books: A Study of College Libraries* (Chicago: American Library Association and Association of American Colleges, 1940).

[20]Peyton Hurt, "The Need of College and University Instruction in Use of the Library," *Library Quarterly* 4 (July 1934):436-84; C.M. Louttit and James R. Patrick, "Study of Student Knowledge in the Use of the Library," *Journal of Applied Psychology* 16 (October 1932):475-84.

[21] Louis Round Wilson, "The Use of the Library in Instruction," in *Proceedings, Institute for Administrative Officers of Higher Education* (Chicago: University of Chicago Press, 1941), 115-27.

[22] Ibid., 124-25.

[23] Barbara H. Phipps, "Library Instruction for the Undergraduate," *College & Research Libraries* 29 (September 1968):411-12.

[24] W. Vance Grant and C. George Lind, *Digest of Educational Statistics, 1973* (Washington, D.C.: Government Printing Office, 1974), 111.

[25] *The Bowker Annual 1970*, ed. Carole Collins and Frank Schick (New York: R.R. Bowker, 1970), 15.

[26] Ibid., 14.

[27] E. Walfred Erickson, "Library Instruction in the Freshman Orientation Program," *College & Research Libraries* 10 (October 1949):445.

[28] Kenneth J. Brough, *Scholar's Workshop: Evolving Conceptions of Library Service* (Urbana: University of Illinois Press, 1953), 159.

[29] Anita R. Schiller, "Reference Services: Instruction or Information," *Library Quarterly* 35 (January 1965):52-60.

[30] Thomas Kirk, "Past, Present, and Future of Library Instruction," *Southeastern Librarian* 27 (Spring 1977):16-17.

[31] Johnnie Givens, "The Use of Resources in the Learning Experience," in *Advances in Librarianship*, vol. 4, ed. Melvin J. Voigt (New York: Academic Press, 1974), 160-64.

[32] Louis Shores, "The College Becomes a Library," *Drexel Library Quarterly* 4 (January 1968):31-44.

[33] Patricia B. Knapp, "A Suggested Program of College Instruction in the Use of the Library," *Library Quarterly* 26 (July 1956):224-31; Patricia B. Knapp, "The Methodology and Results of the Monteith Pilot Project, *Library Trends* 13 (July 1964):84-102.

[34] Phipps, "Library Instruction," 411-12.

35Carnegie Foundation for the Advancement of Teaching, *More Than Survival* (San Francisco: Jossey-Bass, 1975), ix.

36David Kaser, "The Effect of the Revolution of 1969-1970 on University Library Administration," *Academic Libraries by the Year 2000: Essays Honoring Jerrold Orne*, ed. Herbert Poole (New York: R.R. Bowker, 1977), 64.

37Daniel Gore, "The View from the Tower of Babel," *Library Journal* 100 (September 15, 1975):1600.

38James R. Kennedy, Jr., "Integrated Library Instruction," *Library Journal* 95 (April 15, 1970):1450-53.

39Verna V. Melum, "1971 Survey of Library Orientation and Instruction Programs," *Drexel Library Quarterly* 7 (July/October 1971):227.

40Evan I. Farber and Thomas G. Kirk, Jr., "Instruction in Library Use," in *The ALA Yearbook* (Chicago: American Library Association, 1976), 59.

41Evan Ira Farber, "College Librarians and the University-Library Syndrome," in *The Academic Library: Essays in Honor of Guy Lyle*, ed. Evan Ira Farber and Ruth Walling (Metuchen, N.J.: Scarecrow Press, 1974), 12-23.

42Howard W. Dillon, "Organizing the Academic Library for Instruction," *The Journal of Academic Librarianship* 1 (September 1975):4-7.

43Elizabeth Frick, "Information Structure and Bibliographic Instruction," *The Journal of Academic Librarianship* 1 (September 1975):12-14.

44Association of College and Research Libraries, Bibliographic Instruction Section, Policy and Planning Committee, *Bibliographic Instruction Handbook* (Chicago: American Library Association, 1979); Beverly Renford and Linnea Hendrickson, *Bibliographic Instruction: A Handbook* (New York: Neal-Schuman, 1980); James Rice, Jr., *Teaching Library Use* (Westport, Conn.: Greenwood Press, 1981); Anne K. Beaubien, Sharon A. Hogan, and Mary W. George, *Learning the Library: Concepts and Methods for Effective Bibliographic Instruction* (New York: R.R. Bowker, 1982); Anne F. Roberts, *Library Instruction for Librarians* (Littleton, Colo.: Libraries Unlimited, 1982); Cerise Oberman and Katina Strauch, eds. *Theories of Bibliographic Education: Design for Teaching* (New York: R.R. Bowker, 1982); Association of College and Research Libraries, Bibliographic Instruction Section, Subcommittee on Evaluation, *Evaluating Bibliographic Instruction* (Chicago: American Library Association, 1983); Larry L. Hardesty, John P. Schmitt, and John Mark Tucker, eds. *User Instruction in Academic Libraries: A Century of Selected Readings* (Metuchen, N.J.: Scarecrow Press, 1986); Constance Mellon, *Bibliographic Instruction: The Second Generation* (Littleton, Colo.: Libraries Unlimited,

1987); Mary Reichel and Mary A. Ramey, eds. *Conceptual Frameworks for Bibliographic Education: Theory into Practice* (Littleton, Colo.: Libraries Unlimited, 1987).

[45]Farber and Kirk, 59.

[46]Nancy E. Gwinn, "Academic Libraries and Undergraduate Education: The CLR Experience," *College & Research Libraries* 41 (January 1980):5-16.

[47]Arthur P. Young, "And Gladly Teach: Bibliographic Instruction and the Library," in *Advances in Librarianship*, vol. 10, ed. Michael H. Harris (New York: Academic Press, 1980), 80.

[48]Edward G. Holley, "Library Instruction: Some Observations from the Past and Some Questions about the Future," in *Improving Library Instruction: How to Teach and How to Evaluate*, ed. Carolyn A. Kirkendall (Ann Arbor, Mich.: Pierian Press, 1979), 89-96.

[49]William J. Bennett, *To Reclaim a Legacy: A Report on the Humanities in Higher Education* (Washington, D.C.: National Endowment for the Humanities, 1984); Frank Newman, *Higher Education and the American Resurgence* (Princeton, N.J.: Education Commission for the States and the Carnegie Foundation, 1985); The Project on Redefining the Meaning and Purpose of Baccalaureate Degrees, *Integrity in the College Curriculum: A Report to the Academic Community* (Washington, D.C.: Association of American Colleges, 1985); Ernest L. Boyer, *College: A Report on Undergraduate Education in America* (New York: Harper & Row, 1986).

Part IV
KASER AND HIS CONTRIBUTIONS TO LIBRARIANSHIP

8

David Kaser and Sino-American Librarianship

Margaret C. Fung

The establishment of professional librarianship and the enhancement of library service in China since the turn of the century have been instrumental to that nation's development and modernization. From the beginning, one of the principal factors contributing to the improvement of Chinese librarianship has been the involvement of foreign librarians, including American experts. This Sino-American library activity occurred largely in two phases: the first extended approximately from 1910 to 1950, and the second phase began around 1960 and continues today.

No record indicates that any individual has been more involved in the second phase of Sino-American librarianship in the last quarter of a century than David Kaser. In doing so, however, he was following in the footsteps of a number of others who had been active in its first phase, which concentrated on education for librarianship.

FIRST PHASE OF SINO-AMERICAN LIBRARY ACTIVITY

As early as 1913, Harry Clemons, a graduate and librarian of Wesleyan University and Princeton University, introduced library science courses into China at the University of Nanking.[1] Six years later, Mary Elizabeth Wood founded China's first library school, the Boone Library School in Wuhan. Established by an American librarian, this school was supported financially either by Christian missions or American foundations, and its courses were taught by American or American-trained graduates.[2] The Boone Library School aimed at transplanting American systems, methods, and ideas into Chinese library practice.

Many Chinese were also sent on scholarships to the United States for advanced professional training during this period. They either brought back American systems for Chinese rooting or exerted a great impact upon Chinese collections in the United States. These individuals included Hsiu Cha, Kai-ming

Chiu, Chia-pi Hsu, Chin-shen Hu, Hsing-hui Huang, Yu-feng Hung, Chih-ber Kwei, Fang-fu Li, Siao-yuan Li, Kuo-chuin Liu, Ming-hing Mok, Tsu-yung Seng, Tze-chien Tai, Hung-tu Tien, Vi-line Wong, Wen-yu Yen, and Tung-li Yuan.[3]

In December 1947, Charles Harvey Brown, chairman of the American Library Association's (ALA's) Committee on the Orient and Southwest Pacific, and Verner Warren Clapp, Deputy Librarian of Congress, recommended that China should have four additional library schools—at West Union University in Chengtu, at the University of Nanking in Nanking, at National Sun Yat-sen University in Canton, and at National Peking University in Peiping.[4] Their recommendation resulted in the establishment of a library school at the National Peking University.

One of the most profound influences introduced into Chinese librarianship embraced the modern principles of book classification schemes: flexibility, expandability, and inclusiveness. *Dewey Decimal Classification and Relative Index, Library of Congress Classification, Cutter's Expansive Classification,* and Brown's *Subject Classification* were either used as foundations for the revision of Chinese classification or were employed by libraries in classifying their books. Several classification schemes were produced as a result: Tsu-yung Seng's *A System of Classification of Chinese Books Based on Dewey's Classification*, Ding-u Doo's *Universal Classification*, Jih-chang Ho and Yung-chin Yuan's *Decimal Classification for Chinese Books*, Kuo-chuin Liu's *A System of Book Classification for Chinese Libraries*, and Kai-ming Ch'iu's *A Classification Scheme for Chinese and Japanese Books*.[5]

American cataloging rules, such as *ALA Catalog Rules: Author and Title Entries*, Jennie D. Fellows' *Cataloging Rules with Explanation and Illustrations*, Susan G. Akers' *Simple Library Cataloging*, and Theresa Hitchler's *Cataloging for Small Libraries*, were either adopted by Chinese libraries or were used as bases for developing Chinese cataloging rules.[6] The use of subject headings and author numbers can also be attributed to American influence.[7]

Insofar as public services in libraries were concerned, the Boone Library began to introduce such innovations as open shelves, free access, home use, reading guidance, and travelling libraries in 1910.[8] Arthur Elmore Bostwick's visit to China in 1925 inspired the Chinese government with the ideas of modern public libraries and led to the founding of the National Library in Peiping.[9] His visit to fifty libraries in China and his suggestions for practical ways to establish free public libraries in China were instrumental to the development of the Chinese public library system. Many other services, such as interlibrary cooperation and a national union catalog for bibliographical control, were also patterned after American practices.[10]

With the establishment of the China Foundation for Promotion of Education and Culture, and thanks to Mary Elizabeth Wood's efforts, a portion of the Boxer Indemnity Fund was remitted by the United States to China beginning in 1924. This fund would establish and maintain public libraries in China and develop professional librarianship by providing scholarships and professorships to the Boone Library School. In addition, Christian missionary organizations, foundations, and other private donors were major financial supporters.[11]

Regrettably, the library movement in China was halted by the Sino-Japanese war during the period 1939-1945, when many libraries were destroyed.[12] In response to an appeal in 1938 from Tung-li Yuan, chairman of the Executive Committee of the Library Association of China, ALA launched a Books-for-China campaign on June 12, 1938. The association collected 20,000 books, as well as microfilms of selected periodicals and theses to offset the damages.[13] By the end of the 1940s, however, civil war had effectively ended the first phase of Sino-American librarianship.

KASER'S INVOLVEMENT IN THE SECOND PHASE

The above brief historical account exemplifies some of the American efforts that had exerted a significant impact upon the modernization of librarianship in China before 1950. Subsequently, David Kaser's contribution to the development of librarianship in Taiwan has been noteworthy in the following areas:

1. Education and training of librarians
2. Planning for library buildings
3. Sino-American joint understanding of books and libraries

Education and Training of Librarians

David Kaser's personal impact upon Sino-American librarianship began in 1960 when he was appointed director of the Joint University Libraries at Vanderbilt University and Professor of Library Science at Peabody College in Nashville, Tennessee.[14] At that time, several libraries in Taiwan sent young Chinese librarians to study in the master's program at Peabody, where they came into close contact with Kaser and were influenced by his teaching.

Most of these Peabody graduates subsequently became leaders of the Chinese library community, and their efforts toward the advancement of Chinese librarianship since 1960 have been paramount. Yung-hsiang Lai returned to Taiwan to initiate and head the library school at National Taiwan University, which has become the best library school on the island. Lai-lun Chau became the director of the third largest university library, the National Cheng-chih University Library, and built there a modern modular library building. William Chia-chun Ju served as director of the National Central Library, which is now directed by Chen-ku Wang. The National Central Library is charged with providing overall leadership in the development of librarianship, library policies, services, and systems throughout the Republic of China (ROC) on Taiwan. The achievements of Peabody graduates in strengthening the professional associations, promoting professional publications, formulating library standards and legislation, enhancing professional education, and advocating interlibrary cooperation in Taiwan must be partly attributed to the education, guidance, and inspiration those graduates acquired in Kaser's lectures.

Dr. Chiang Fu-tsung, who devoted his entire life to the collection, preservation, and dissemination of Chinese culture through his directorship of the National Central Library (1933-1966) and of the National Palace Museum (1966-1982), visited Kaser in Nashville during the fall of 1960.[15] This brief visit resulted in a lasting professional friendship between Chiang and Kaser that has extended over almost three decades. These two dedicated professionals spoke the same professional language and shared the same professional aspirations, even though they were unable to speak each other's native tongue. Some of Chiang's proposals, ideas, and endeavors for the blueprints and policies of library services in Taiwan coincided with the long-range planning and administrative efforts advocated by Kaser. It was partly Chiang's dedication to Chinese librarianship that earned Kaser's constant support for library professionalism in China. Chiang respected Kaser as a scholar and a librarian of vision and wisdom: "It is commendable," he remarked recently, "that Dr. Kaser devotes much effort to the promotion of international understanding through librarianship with his keen observation, far-sightedness and wisdom. Chinese librarians have benefitted greatly from his various endeavors in the field.[16]

Between 1968 and 1973, Kaser was the Director of Libraries at Cornell University. His duties, his interactions with faculty members and students, and his oversight of the important Wason Collection of Sinology put him into constant contact with Chinese librarians, students, and scholars in many parts of the world.

During his teaching career at the School of Library and Information Science at Indiana University since 1973, David Kaser taught and advised many Chinese students from both sides of the Taiwan straits, as well as from Hong Kong, Singapore, Malaysia, and other parts of the Orient. Several Chinese are among Kaser's doctoral graduates: Robert Pin-chuan Chen, currently professor/ coordinator of Documents Services at Eastern Illinois University; Mei-hua Yang, librarian of Feng-chia University in Taichung; and Margaret C. Fung, currently conducting research under the affiliation of a research associateship at Harvard University and serving as advisor to several cultural and library projects in Taiwan and in the United States. Robert Pin-chuan Chen's project, "Library Resources for American Studies in Taiwan: An Evaluation," Mei-hua Yang's dissertation on Chinese education for librarianship entitled "Library Educational Personnel Planning in ROC on Taiwan," and Margaret C. Fung's research on the topic "Evolving Social Mission of the National Central Library 1928-1966" all received Kaser's undivided attention and guidance from beginning to end.[17] All of them have expressed gratitude for his guidance, patience, support, care, enthusiasm, and encouragement.[18] He was never too busy for his students or turned any of them away, but rather he treated their projects as if they were his very own and literally labored with them during the course of research. This professional integrity and dedication served them as examples to follow throughout their careers. With Kaser's advice and support, they, too, have been continuously working for the betterment of Sino-American librarianship since their graduation.

As a historian, David Kaser has long been interested in the evolution of Chinese libraries. He became especially interested in the efforts of Dr. Tung-li Yuan to develop librarianship in China during the middle of this century. With the encouragement of Yuan's family, Kaser was instrumental in establishing the Yuan Tung-li Memorial Scholarship Fund in the School of Library and Information Science at Indiana University. Since 1983 Kuo-chun Chen, Lily Wee, and Hsiu-ying Chiang have received this scholarship.[19] Since this scholarship is an endowed fund, Chinese librarianship will benefit from it in perpetuity, in recognition of Yuan Tung-li's contributions to the Chinese library profession. Already the above-mentioned recipients have successfully completed their studies at Indiana University; Chen and Chiang returned to Taipei to serve the libary community at the National Institute of the Arts and National Central Library, while Wee devotes herself to the academic library profession in the United States.

In addition to the students David Kaser taught in the United States, librarians in Taiwan and other parts of the world have learned a great deal from his lectures and publications on Chinese libraries. His first lecture at National Taiwan University in 1967 exerted a profound influence upon faculty members and students of that newly established library school.[20] Also at National Taiwan University, in November 1969, Kaser lectured on some of the persistent problems of international librarianship.[21] Meanwhile his speech entitled "Humanism, the Library and Quality of Life," delivered at the Chinese-American Librarians Association meeting in River Forest, Illinois on May 10, 1975, inspired Chinese librarians in the United States and they responded to his talk with enthusiasm.[22]

In November 1979 Kaser was invited to participate in a continuing education workshop, "Library Planning and Media Technology" at National Taiwan Normal University.[23] More than 200 practicing librarians from all parts of Taiwan participated in the workshop and were inspired by the principles of participatory management, the importance of identifying goals, missions, and objectives for library services, and the planning guidelines for modern library buildings. The series of lectures opened up a new horizon to Chinese library administrators and practitioners and greatly enriched many of the planning efforts of libraries in Taiwan. When the proceedings were published in 1980, they were in great demand and were widely distributed.

On December 2, 1979, Kaser addressed the Library Association of China assembly at Taipei in a speech entitled "Why Libraries Indeed?" He emphasized the importance of knowing the *why* of library services and librarians' duties rather than the traditional *how*.[24] In another lecture at National Central Library in Taipei three years later, he also stressed the impact of modern technology upon library services and the ways in which librarians must prepare themselves for the twenty-first century.[25] On these occasions, in recognition of his contributions to Sino-American librarianship, he was presented with plaques by the National Taiwan Normal University, the Library Association of China, and the National Central Library.

As part of the observance of Captive Nations Week in 1982, Kaser was invited by the World Anti-Communist League to present a talk at National Taiwan Normal University on July 20. In his address, "Free Knowledge or Fettered Minds," he outlined the importance of intellectual freedom, especially with regard to books and libraries, citing historical examples that illustrated the reasons why attempts to suppress ideas are inevitably self-defeating.[26] Here, as on many other occasions, his audience was not limited to practitioners in the field of library and information science. His talks at the Institute of Chinese Architects at National Taiwan Normal University on December 1, 1979, and at the ROC Chapter of the Indiana University Alumni Association on March 25, 1982, reached a large and varied audience.[27]

David Kaser has continuously paid attention to the promotion of professional understanding among American and Chinese librarians on both the professional and personal level. Most of the Chinese librarians who have attended conferences of professional associations in the United States have had the pleasure of meeting him because he makes an effort to become acquainted with foreign librarians. One particular case deserves recording. In October 1982, after the American Society for Information Science Conference in Chicago, Harris B.H. Seng (professor of library science, National Taiwan University), Jack Kai-tung Huang (Ming-chuan College), and Margaret C. Fung (professor of library science, National Taiwan Normal University) went to visit Indiana University. Kaser drove back and forth four times between Indianapolis and Bloomington (a total of more than 200 miles) within twelve hours to meet these foreign friends. He and Mrs. Kaser showed them the warmest American hospitality by inviting all the faculty members of the library school, university faculty members of Chinese descent, and Chinese students in the library school to meet them in their home. "This meeting was most impressive and beneficial to faculty members," Seng observed later. "It furthered cooperation and understanding between Chinese and American librarians and information scientists."[28]

Planning for Library Buildings

David Kaser also has exerted an important influence upon the planning of library buildings in Taiwan. In 1979 his address to the Institute of Chinese Architects on planning for modern library buildings helped architects there to understand the special specifications, criteria, and needs of an academic library building. The timing of this lecture was particularly opportune because the Taiwan area's economy was then expanding and the ROC was implementing an extensive Cultural Planning and Development Program. As a result, there was a great need for constructing functional library buildings. When Kaser was invited to consult on the design of a new library building at the National Taiwan Normal University in the same year, he pointed out to the university administrators and to Ying-hsuan Peng, the architect, both the desirable and undesirable features of modern academic library structures.[29]

The ROC government's efforts to launch a wide range of cultural and educational projects resulted in the establishment of the new National Institute of the Arts in 1982. As a new institution of higher learning, this institute's faculty and staff members, under the preparatory guidance of its director, Yao-yu Bao, realized the importance of a library to meet the educational, informational, and instructional needs of its four departments. At the invitation of the institute, Kaser made a special trip to Taipei in March 1982 for consultation with the well-known Chinese architect C.Y. Lee. Their meetings on the design of a new library building for that institution produced a functional library blueprint. Yao-yu Bao particularly appreciated Kaser's assistance and stated:

> Dr. Kaser's insights into the importance of the close relationship between culture and the library have been extremely valuable to us in designing our new library. He always takes the cultural uniqueness of each institution and country into consideration when he is asked to consult on the library buildings. I have been greatly impressed by this concern. We have adapted his ideas of a functional library and we also added additional quarters for an art museum behind the library. This hybrid building resulted from his strong advocacy for the close relationship between culture and library building.[30]

Lee thought that Kaser's practical principles set for the academic library building were indeed helpful:

> Dr. Kaser insisted on air-conditioning, carpets, and a mixture of books and readers in order best to preserve the library collection and to provide easy accessibility and comfort to the users.[31]

When construction was just begun on the fine new National Central Library (NCL) building, the architect, Pau-sen Chen, and his associates went to Bloomington, Indiana on December 17, 1983. Their specific purpose was to discuss the project and the plans with Kaser. Chen-ku Wang, director of the NCL, and Pau-sen Chen recalled Kaser's concern over the relationship of cultural assets and national heritage. This idea about the library building reinforced their conviction that the NCL's new library building plans should indeed reflect the close relationship between the Chinese cultural heritage and the future development of the library. The NCL building is designed for people—the readers, staff, and other users—as well as for the book collection. Its rich 858,158-volume collection and spacious 443,000-square-foot building strive to: (1) achieve coordination and integrity between the parts and the entirety, (2) provide abundant information through the use of modern technological facilities, and (3) present the inner cultural heritage through the symbolic subtlety of the new building layouts.[32]

In addition, NCL director Chen-ku Wang expressed appreciation for Kaser's publications on library buildings, including his draft of a library building program for the National Institute of the Arts, which is required reading for library building seminar courses taught in graduate library schools in Taipei. Kaser's article on academic library buildings published in *College and Research Libraries* (July 1984) was translated into Chinese and the Chinese translation was published in Taipei in the *Journal of Library and Information Science*.[33] It is likely that it too will assist in solidifying Kaser's influence on library building planning in the ROC.

Sino-American Joint Understanding of Books and Libraries

Doubtlessly, David Kaser's most substantive contribution to Sino-American understanding came when he brought his expertise in publishing history to bear upon a serious problem in book trade relations between the two countries. The unauthorized reprinting, usually called "piracy," of English-language books in the ROC had aroused international attention and dispute since the early 1950s.

In 1966 Kaser, then director of the Vanderbilt University Libraries, stopped in Taipei en route from a tour of duty in Korea with the United States Agency for International Development's contract studying the needs and capabilities of the Korean book industry. During this visit to Taiwan, he encountered modern book piracy for the first time and immediately became impressed with its similarities to the American pirates of British publications in the nineteenth century.[34] Accordingly, he returned to Taiwan twice in 1967 as a Guggenheim Fellow to investigate this phenomenon. In 1969 the University of Pennsylvania Press published Kaser's report entitled *Book Pirating in Taiwan*.[35] This research turned out to be important to both the book trade and government circles in the United States and on Taiwan.

Through access to both American and Chinese private and governmental files, and through interviews with publishers, booksellers, government officials, educators, and others in the United States, Taiwan, Hong Kong, Japan, Macao, Korea, and the Philippines, Kaser documented the entire issue and pinpointed its problems. His report was viewed as a systematic, unbiased, scholarly investigation, and it won instant popularity and exerted its due impact. Two weeks after its appearance in Philadelphia, it was legally reprinted by the Mei Ya Publishing Company of Taipei. This work expedited remedial measures taken by the governments and book industries of both countries.

In a book review article, Chi-wu Wang, a renowned social scientist, commented on Kaser's work. "This book is not only important to the study of contemporary Chinese cultural history but is also a pivotal resource for the study of Sino-American relations."[36] Kaser pointed out that psychological and behavioral problems prevented a resolution of the American and Chinese publishers' dispute. No political, economic, or legal difficulties were involved. This book provided the foundation for understanding and mutual trust.

Sueling Li, the Chinese who has been more diligent than anyone else in seeking a resolution to the problem, commented on the significance of Kaser's work as follows:

> Dr. Kaser, in 1967, researched and vividly authored *Book Pirating in Taiwan*—a masterpiece of documentary recording never seen before on the English-language book industry in Taiwan, as opposed to the Chinese-language industry there.

He examined the governmental aspects, like the Republic of China on Taiwan not being a member of a world copyright convention; local laws not being able to protect a foreign work against piracy until the work is copyrighted and licensed in Taiwan; local customs not being able to curb smugglers from smuggling books out; the 1903 U.S./China Treaty giving ... to the Chinese people free rights to translate any English-language work of American authorship, and so forth.

Dr. Kaser discreetly used such terms as "unauthorized reprinting" instead of "literary piracy," in view of the local circumstances. He urged the local trade to apply for authorization and to pay royalties. He urged U.S. copyright proprietors to grant rights to requests and locally register copyright for local protection. He knew that this educational process to recognize and respect intellectual property rights would take time. Through Dr. Kaser's enlightening disclosure, governments' new actions, and the incessant practice of authorized publishing ... by Mei Ya Publications, Inc., there is definite evidence of improvements towards eliminating book pirating in Taiwan, even though a handful of unscrupulous and incorrigible business people still operate in the market. The cure may be faster if Dr. Kaser would update his work again soon.[37]

Tun-sheng Hsiung, president of Chung Hwa Book Company, who was directly involved in the dispute, recently made the following comments:

Dr. Kaser's book collected detailed information and provides [an] in-depth description of the actual status of the problem of intellectual property in Taiwan. It presents factual information on how and what [the] U.S. and Chinese government[s] did in helping to stop illegal reprinting. It is not only the most comprehensive and accurate report but also serves as an inspiration to the Chinese government as well as Chinese academicians. It enhances the Chinese government's [and] civilians' understanding ...[of] the importance of intellectual property. Through Dr. Kaser's work, they have been led to understand that the protection of intellectual property is essential to the nation's development. As a result, laws have been revised for the purpose of building up the protection of intellectual property. Dr. Kaser's work was completed twenty years ago, but its influence and contribution to the solution of illegal reprints have indeed been tremendous and should be recognized.[38]

Basil Dandison, former senior vice president of the McGraw-Hill Company, commented in a recent interview on Kaser's work as follows:

He gave a well-balanced view to the subject. His comprehensive treatment of the problem not only has given guidance to the United States of America and Taiwanese publishers but also has given recognition to the protection of authors. His thoughtful contribution has alerted all the parties involved in the matter to rethink the long-range needs and work toward the establishment of a reasonable solution. We all are deeply indebted to David Kaser for his work.[39]

This remark was also supported by Leo Albert, president of Prentice-Hall International.[40] After thirty years' dispute, revision of the copyright laws was announced by then ROC President Chiang Ching-kuo on July 10, 1985.[41] To the degree that there is law and order in the book reprinting business in Taipei today, Kaser's effort must be credited.

In addition to his important work on book pirating in Taiwan, David Kaser also wrote and lectured extensively on both sides of the Pacific, seeking better mutual understanding. Important to both the American and Chinese library communities are his presentation "Books and Libraries in the Far East," given to the ALA Armed Forces Librarians meeting on June 24, 1968;[42] his article "Books for International Studies";[43] his report "Library Development in the Republic of China";[44] his talk, "Organizing an Oriental Collection," at an ALA gathering on July 1, 1970 in Detroit;[45] his article "Library Development in Asia," published in the 1972 edition of *Encyclopedia Americana*;[46] and his work on the significance of libraries, published in *Journal of Library and Information Science* in 1980.[47]

Kaser's effort in reporting the status of Chinese libraries to an American audience deserves special recognition. His book entitled *Library Development in Eight Asian Countries* (1969), in which the ROC was thoroughly presented, was for a long time considered the best survey of the topic available in English.[48]

CONCLUSION

All enterprises in the world are interdependent and librarianship is no exception. Like other professionals preceding him, David Kaser's efforts are deeply rooted in Chinese-American librarianship; their legacy is impressive and their impact is lasting.

Kaser's most recent contribution to Sino-American librarianship is expressed through his concern over the need for the ROC to establish a well-balanced national information policy. This concern indeed reflects his enduring care for China.[49]

This discussion has given a bird's-eye view of one scholar-librarian's contribution to international librarianship through the documentation of his efforts in support of Sino-American librarianship. In these labors, Kaser has always emphasized the importance of "adaptation," rather than "adoption," of library practices when they are introduced from one country to another. This is sage advice for librarians working on the international front.

David Kaser's own comments on his endeavors in Sino-American librarianship well illustrate his professional dedication to international librarianship, which few people can surpass:

There were great differences in the library principles and practices of East and West a century ago when Kipling opined that "Never the twain shall meet." Time, however, has proved him to be wrong. Thanks to extensive trans-Pacific bibliothecal contact and mutual exploration over the decades, there are today many remarkable library similarities and a strong sense of professional community binding together the librarians of the United States and the Republic of China on Taiwan. The experience, I believe, provides compelling evidence of the universal brotherhood of man.[50]

NOTES

[1] Fu-ts'ung Chiang, "Chung-kuo t'u shu kuan kuan yuan ti chiao yu wen t'i," *Chung kuo t'u shu kuan hsueh hui hui pao* (Bulletin of Chinese Library Association) 1 (December 1960):1.

[2] Tsu-yung Seng, "Professional Training of Librarianship in China," in *Libraries in China* (Peiping: Library Association of China, 1935), 60; *Ti i tz'u Chung kuo chiao yu nien chien* (The Education Yearbook, First Issue) (Shanghai: Kaiming Shu Chu, 1934), 786; *Ti erh tz'u Chung-kuo chiao yu nien chien* (The Education Yearbook, Second Issue) (Shanghai: Commercial Press, 1948), 1114; George Huang, "Miss Elizabeth Wood: Pioneer of the Library Movement in China," *Journal of Library and Information Science* 1 (April 1979):72.

[3] Chih-chun Tien Au, "American Impact on Modern Chinese Library Development" (Master's thesis, University of Chicago, 1964), 27-40.

[4] Verner Warren Clapp, "Visit to China," *Library of Congress Information Bulletin* (March 1948):7.

[5] Tsien-hsuin Tsien, "A History of Bibliographic Classification in China," *Library Quarterly* 22 (October 1952):318, 321-22; Yuan-ch'ing Chiang, *Chung kuo t'u shu fen lei chih yen ko* (History of Chinese Book Classification) (Shanghai: Chung Hua Shu Chu, 1937), 207-8, 214-21; Kaiming Chiu, "Classification in China," *Library Journal* 52 (April 1927):409-14.

[6] Kuang-tsing Wu, "Ten Years of Classification and Cataloging in China," in *Libraries in China* (Peiping: Library Association of China, 1935), 47-48.

[7] Hsiu Cha, "Chung wen shu chi pien mu wen t'i," *Hsin Chiao Yu* (New Education) 9 (September 1924): 191-207.

[8] Tsung-yung Seng, "Can the American Library System Be Adopted to China?" *Library Journal* 41 (June 1916):388.

⁹Arthur Bostwick, "Report of Arthur E. Bostwick's Mission to China as ALA Delegate," *American Library Association Bulletin* 11 (October 1926):41.

¹⁰Chih-chun Tien Au, "American Impact on Modern Chinese Library Development," (Master's Thesis, University of Chicago,1964), 27-40.

¹¹Ibid., 49-52.

¹²*Ti erh tz'u Chung kuo chiao yu nien chien* (The Education Yearbook, Second Issue) (Shanghai: Commercial Press, 1948), 1115; Tung-li Yuan, "Library Situation in China," *Library Journal* 69 (March 1944):235-38.

¹³J. P. Danton, "Books for China," *Library Journal* 63 (October 1938):714; Tung-li Yuan, "Library Situation in China," *Library Journal* 69 (March 1944):237.

¹⁴David Kaser, notes to author, December 6, 1986.

¹⁵Ibid.

¹⁶Fu-tsung Chiang, interview with author, Taipei, Taiwan, August 13, 1987.

¹⁷Robert Pin-chuan Chen, *Library Resources for American Studies in Taiwan: An Evaluation* (Taipei: The American Studies Association of the Republic of China, 1979); Mei-hua Yang, "Library Educational Personnel Planning in ROC on Taiwan," (Ph.D. diss., Indiana University, 1986); Margaret C. Fung, *The Evolving Social Mission of the National Central Library* (Ann Arbor, Mich.: University Microfilms, 1983).

¹⁸Robert Pin-chuan Chen to Herbert S. White, letter, June 17, 1985; Margaret C. Fung to Herbert S. White, letter, June 5, 1985, in support of Dr. Kaser's nomination for the title of Distinguished Professor.

¹⁹Barbara Dewey, letter to author, July 24, 1987.

²⁰David Kaser, notes to author, December 6, 1986.

²¹David Kaser, "Problems in International Librarianship," *National Taiwan University Library Science Circular* 18 (November 1969):1-7; reprinted in *Library Progress* 3 (1970):77-82.

²²David Kaser, "Humanism, the Library and the Quality of Life," *Journal of Library and Information Science* 1 (October 1975):25-35.

²³*Library Workshop Proceedings, December 28-30, 1979* (Taipei: National Taiwan Normal University, 1980).

[24]David Kaser, "Why Libraries Indeed?" *Chung-kuo t'u shu kuan hsueh hui hui pao* (Library Association of China Bulletin) 31 (December 1979):110-12; David Kaser, "Why Libraries Indeed?" *National Central Library Newsletter* 11 (January 1980):86-91.

[25]David Kaser, "Preparing for the 21st Century Library," *Library Association of China Newsletter* 30 (July 1982):9-12.

[26]David Kaser, "Free Knowledge or Fettered Minds," *Journal of Library and Information Science* 9 (April 1983):19-26.

[27]"Dr. Kaser Lectures before Librarians," *China Post*, March 25, 1982; Institute of Chinese Architects Announcement, November 1979.

[28]Harris B.H. Seng, interview with author, Taipei, Taiwan, August 17, 1987.

[29]National Taiwan Normal University library files, November 26, 1979.

[30]Yao-yu Bao, interview with author, Taipei, Taiwan, August 13, 1987.

[31]C.Y. Lee, interview with author, Taipei, Taiwan, August 18, 1987.

[32]Chen-ku Wang, interview with author, Taipei, Taiwan, August 12, 1987; Pau-sen Chen, interview with author, Taipei, Taiwan, August 18, 1987.

[33]Chen-ku Wang, interview with author, Taipei, Taiwan, August 12, 1987; David Kaser, "Erh shi wu nien lai mei kuo hsueh shu t'u shu kuan kuan she chih kwei hua," ("Twenty-Five Years of American Academic Library Building Planning," originally published in July 1984 issue of *College & Research Libraries*; translated into Chinese by Margaret C. Fung) *Journal of Library and Information Science* 12 (October 1986):240-51.

[34]David Kaser, *Messrs. Carey and Lea of Philadelphia: A Study in the History of the Book Trade* (Philadelphia: University of Pennsylvania Press, 1957).

[35]David Kaser, *Book Pirating in Taiwan* (Philadelphia: University of Pennsylvania Press, 1969).

[36]Chi-wu Wang, "Fan ying yang shu ti lai lung chu mo" (The Accounts of Foreign Book Reprints), *Tsung ho yueh k'an* (October 1969):85.

[37]Sueling Li, letter to author, August 1, 1987.

[38]Tun-sheng Hsiung's comments made at the request of Sueling Li on July 24, 1987, during Hsiung's visit to Chicago, Illinois.

[39]Basil Dandison, letter to author, July 11, 1987.

⁴⁰Leo Alpert, telephone interview with author, July 9, 1987.

⁴¹*Ts'ung t'ung fu kung pao* (Presidential Office Gazette) 4475, July 10, 1985.

⁴²David Kaser, "Books and Libraries in the Far East," *Wilson Library Bulletin* 43 (June 1969):974-79.

⁴³David Kaser, "Books for International Studies," *Cornell University International Studies Bulletin* 2 (May 1971):1-2; (Alumni Issue, 1971):2-3.

⁴⁴David Kaser, "Library Development in the Republic of China," *National Taiwan University Library Science Circular* 14 (May 1969):1-14.

⁴⁵David Kaser, "Organizing an Oriental Collection, *Foreign Acquisitions Newsletter* 33 (Spring 1971):2-5.

⁴⁶*Encyclopedia Americana*, international ed., s.v. "library development in Asia," by David Kaser.

⁴⁷David Kaser, "Significance of Libraries: Four Cases," *Journal of Library and Information Science* 6 (October 1980):131-39.

⁴⁸David Kaser, C. Walter Stone, and Cecil K. Byrd, *Library Development in Eight Asian Countries* (Metuchen, N.J.: Scarecrow Press, 1969), 72-88.

⁴⁹Hui-hsing Lu, "Yu yuan ti, yu ying ti, wo meng huan shu hsiang i hsiang; wei shih mo yao wei t'u shu kuan fei hsin fei li?" (When we have hardware and software, we have to think what efforts we have to contribute to librarianship), *Mensheng Daily News*, September 3, 1983.

⁵⁰David Kaser, note to author, July 31, 1987.

ADDITIONAL READINGS

"Chung hua chiao yu kai chin she ti erh chieh nien hui pao kao, T'u shu kuan chiao yu tsu." *Hsin chiao-yu* (New Education) 68 (October 1923):305.

Institute of Chinese Architects Announcement, November 1979.

Kaser, David. "National Institute of the Arts Program Requirements for the Library Building, 28 March 1982" (mimeographed).

National Institute of the Arts. Correspondence file (January 20, 1982; February 12, 1982; February 26, 1982).

9

David Kaser
A Biographical Sketch

Joanne E. Passet

David Kaser is the senior library historian of his generation and one of the most prominent academic librarians of his time. Moreover, he has inspired several generations of students through his sound scholarship and lively, spirited teaching. His international consultancies have shaped numerous library buildings and enhanced many students' learning environments. Indeed, he has had a substantial impact upon the profession of librarianship.

THE EARLY YEARS

Kaser was born in Mishawaka, Indiana, on March 12, 1924, the son of Arthur LeRoy and Loah (Steele) Kaser, the grandson of northern Indiana farmers. His father had a lifelong enthusiasm for the theater and devoted much of his life to writing for the amateur stage. Because young Kaser lived virtually on the border of Indiana and Michigan, he attended Niles High School in Michigan, where he was active in theater and musical groups and lettered in track and cross-country. Voted "Most Popular Boy" in the school, young Kaser also worked twenty hours each week at a soda fountain.

After graduating from high school in 1941, he enrolled in North Georgia College, but his studies were interrupted two years later when he was conscripted into the United States Army. Kaser served with the Armored Forces and saw combat in the European/African/Middle Eastern campaign. He also served in the Alaskan theatre. The soldier was a voracious reader and carried a copy of the *Pocket Book of English Verse* in the turret of his tank. The volume finally fell apart, but by that time he had memorized many of the poems that he would, years later, quote during his lectures to library school students.

Kaser spent his last year of military service as an army recruiter, and then he enrolled in Houghton College in New York to complete his undergraduate education. He would dedicate his first book, *Messrs. Carey and Lea of Philadelphia*, to Ray W. Hazlett, his English professor at Houghton. While working on his undergraduate degree, Kaser became a student assistant in the cataloging department of the college library, working under the supervision of

Jane Jewell, who subsequently became his wife. The two married in September 1950, a year after Kaser received his B.A. in English from Houghton. Elected to *Who's Who Among Students in American Colleges and Universities* in 1949, he would be listed in *Who's Who in America* only eight years later. Next, Kaser completed an M.A. in English at the University of Notre Dame, working under the direction of the Reverend Chester Soletta, C.S.C.

THE MIDDLE YEARS

In 1950 the Kasers moved to Ann Arbor, where, in addition to doing further work in English, he completed an A.M.L.S. and a Ph.D. in the School of Library Science at the University of Michigan. Although William Warner Bishop had retired several years earlier, he remained an influential figure on campus. Kaser, who did not want to forgo scholarship when he became a librarian, regarded this keen scholar and successful library administrator as a role model. By the time Kaser completed his doctoral dissertation under the direction of Rudolph Gjelsness, he had already begun his career in librarianship, serving as serials librarian and instructor in library science at Ball State Teachers College, and as an assistant in exchange at the University of Michigan. Among the early courses he taught were History of Books and Printing and Research Methods. In 1956 he went to Washington University in St. Louis as chief of acquisitions, where he later became assistant director of libraries for technical services under Andrew Eaton.

David Kaser remained at Washington University until 1960, when he relinquished his position to become the director of the pioneering Joint University Libraries at Vanderbilt University and professor of library science at George Peabody College in Nashville, Tennessee. During his eight years at Vanderbilt, Kaser was able to initiate a substantial collection development program and to oversee the addition of a large wing to the central library building. While at Vanderbilt, David and Jane became the parents of two children, John (now a librarian) and Kathleen.

Kaser left Nashville in 1968 to assume the directorship of the prestigious Cornell University Libraries. While at Cornell, he continued his involvement in library education, teaching in the area of library administration at Syracuse University. A festschrift prepared by his Cornell colleagues when Kaser left the directorship five years later acknowledged the library director's role as a catalyst for change. Not only had he precipitated much intellectual growth among Cornell University librarians and staff, but he had also emphasized development of the individual. While at Cornell, Kaser initiated activity toward the Lafayette Papers Project, led one of the very early exercises in strategic planning (with funding from the Council on Library Resources, and guidance from the American Management Association's Center for Planning), and continued the enhancement of area studies programs, especially those focusing on East and Southeast Asia.

Kaser's next move was to Indiana University, where he accepted a position in the Graduate Library School (now the School of Library and Information Science) in 1973.

David Kaser has also pursued an active consulting career, serving in advisory capacities on four continents. Since 1958 he has traveled the globe in his role as a building and space consultant, advising more than 130 institutions in Canada, Indonesia, Korea, Nigeria, Saudi Arabia, Taiwan, and the United States. One of his consultancies, the St. Mary's College Library of Notre Dame, received the AIA/ALA Award, and he is proud of his work for the library at Ewha Women's University in Seoul, Korea, the largest women's university in the world. Beginning in 1964 he also became involved with consultancies not related to building matters, and other foreign assignments have included visits to Burma, Cambodia, France, Ireland, Japan, and Vietnam. This worldwide involvement has led Kaser to consider himself a "library citizen of the world."

SUMMARY OF HONORS AND ACHIEVEMENTS

The profession has recognized David Kaser's abilities at both the national and international levels. The membership of the American Library Association (ALA) has twice elected him an ALA Councilor, and he has held the presidencies of the Association of College and Research Libraries, Beta Phi Mu, and the Tennessee Library Association. Additional honors include grants from the American Philosophical Society, the Asia Foundation, the Council on Library Resources, the National Historical Publications Commission, and the Pacific Cultural Foundation. One of only five Guggenheim Fellows selected from the field of librarianship, he also was elected to Phi Beta Kappa in 1969. The University of Michigan School of Library Science honored him as a distinguished alumnus in 1970, and Indiana University recognized him with a Distinguished Teaching Award in 1981. In April 1986, Indiana University honored the prominent library educator by conferring on him the title Distinguished Professor, one of that institution's highest honors.

David Kaser is one of the senior library historians in the country and has published widely on historical subjects as well as on literary, administrative, and architectural topics. His fourteen monographs and more than two hundred articles have added significantly to our understanding of the library profession and its history (see appendix B). Indeed, four of his books are listed in the *Harvard Guide to American History*. In addition to being a productive scholar, Kaser has served in editorial capacities with the *Missouri Library Association Quarterly, Library Resources and Technical Services*, and *College & Research Libraries*. His quality research, his perceptive interpretations, and his lucid writing stand as models for scholars of librarianship.

Not only is David Kaser an exemplary scholar, but he has also shared his knowledge and editorial skills with students who, benefiting from his guidance and example, are also making noteworthy contributions to the professional literature. Newly enrolled students at the Indiana University School of Library and Information Science are advised (often by other students) to include at least one "Kaser course" in their program. These courses include History of the Book, History of American Libraries, The Academic Library, and International Librarianship. Furthermore, while at Indiana, David Kaser has guided the work of numerous doctoral students, directing more than forty Ph.D. dissertations on subjects ranging from the history of mosque libraries in Islamic life and culture, to the social mission of the National Central Library in Taiwan, to the role of personnel offices in academic libraries (see appendix C). Since 1974 Kaser's annual "Feast of Saint Lawrence," held in honor of the patron saint of libraries, has been one of the social highlights of the summer. There is little doubt that David Kaser is regarded with great affection by his students, both past and present, who recognize that one of the greatest gifts he has given them is the gift of time.

David Kaser's positive outlook on life has encouraged, motivated, and energized those with whom he has come in contact. This festschrift stands as a tribute to a dynamic man, whose intellectual vigor and natural enthusiasm have instilled in countless students and colleagues a joy for life and pride in their chosen profession.

The following sources were consulted in preparing this biographical sketch.

"David Kaser," in Guy R. Lyle, ed. *The Librarian Speaking* (Athens: University of Georgia Press, 1970), 57-70; "Dr. Kaser Honored," *Alumni Newsletter* (Indiana University School of Library and Information Science) 26 (Summer 1986): 1; Houghton College *Boulder*, 1949; "The Kaser Years, 1968-1973," Special Issue, Cornell University Libraries *Bulletin* (July 1973); David Kaser, "Arthur L. Kaser; Gag Man for the Amateur," *Books at Brown* 18 (March 1958): 94-115; David Kaser, *Books and Libraries in Camp and Battle: The Civil War Experience* (Westport, Conn.: Greenwood Press, 1984); Niles (Michigan) High School *Tattler*, 1941; personal papers in the possession of David Kaser, Bloomington, Indiana; and personal interview, October 15, 1988.

APPENDIXES

Appendix A
A David Kaser Chronology

1924 (March 12)	Born Mishawaka, Indiana
1942-1943	Attends North Georgia College
1943-1946	U.S. Army (Armored Forces), Alaskan and European Theatres
1947-1949	Attends Houghton College
1948-1949	Library Assistant, Houghton College
1949	B.A. in English, Houghton College
1950	Marries Jane A. Jewell
1950	M.A. in English, University of Notre Dame
1952	M.L.S., University of Michigan
1952-1954	Periodical Services Librarian and Instructor, Ball State Teachers College
1954-1956	Assistant in Exchange, University of Michigan
1956	Ph.D., University of Michigan
1956-1959	Chief of Acquisitions, Washington University
1957	*Messrs. Carey and Lea of Philadelphia*
1958	American Philosophical Society Grant
1958	*Washington University Manuscripts*, with Jane Kaser
1958-1960	Editor, *Missouri Library Association Quarterly*
1958-1962	BSA, Regional Advisory Board
1958-1962	Assistant Editor, *Library Resources and Technical Services*
1959-1960	Assistant Director, Washington University
1960	American Philosophical Society Research Grant

1960	Chairman, American Library Association, RTSD Acquisitions Section
1960-1968	Professor, George Peabody College
1960-1968	Director of Libraries, Joint University Libraries, Vanderbilt University
1960-present	*Who's Who in America*
1961	Chairman, American Library Association, ACRL University Libraries Section
1961	Compiler, *Directory of St. Louis Book and Printing Trades to 1850*
1963	*Joseph Charless, Printer in the Western Country*
1963	Editor, *The Cost Book of Carey and Lea*
1963-1969	Editor, *College and Research Libraries*
1964	Chairman, Southeastern Library Association, College and University Library Section
1965-1969	Councilor, American Library Association
1966	Compiler, *Directory of the Printing and Related Industries in Ante-Bellum Nashville*
1966	*Developmental Book Activities and Needs in the Republic of Korea*, with S. A. Barnett, C. W. Stone, and E. H. Michener
1966	Editor, *Books in America's Past; Essays Honoring Rudolph Gjelsness*
1966-1968	Chair, Association of Southeastern Research Libraries
1967	Guggenheim Foundation Fellow
1967	*Developmental Book Activities and Needs in Laos*, with S. A. Barnett and E. Brown
1968-1969	President, Association of College and Research Libraries
1968-1969	President, Tennessee Library Association
1968-1973	Director of Libraries, Cornell University
1969	Elected Phi Beta Kappa
1969	*Book Pirating in Taiwan*
1969	*Library Development in Eight Asian Countries*

1969-1972	Member, Board of Directors, Association of Research Libraries
1969-1972	Lecturer in Library Science, Syracuse University
1970	Distinguished Alumnus, University of Michigan School of Library Science
1970	Council on Library Resources Grant
1971	Asia Foundation Grant
1971	National Historical Publications Commission Grant
1972	National Historical Publications Commission Grant
1972	President, Universal Book and Serial Exchange (USBE)
1972	Council on Library Resources Grant
1973-present	Professor, School of Library and Information Science, Indiana University
1974	Council on Library Resources Grant
1975	President, Beta Phi Mu
1975-1979	Councilor, American Library Association
1977	*The Viability of Merging Three Academic Libraries in Worcester*, with Jinnie Y. Davis
1979	Pacific Cultural Foundation Grant
1980	*A Book for a Sixpence*
1981	Asia Foundation Grant
1981	Distinguished Teaching Award, Indiana University
1984	*Books in Camp and Battle*
1986	Named Distinguished Professor, Indiana University
1989	Celebrates sixty-fifth birthday

Appendix B
A Chronology of Publications by David Kaser

1950
"The Language of Leigh Hunt's Poetry." Master's thesis, University of Notre Dame, 1950.

1955
"Have Winchell; Will Travel." *Wilson Library Bulletin* 30 (November 1955): 263-64.

"Two New Leigh Hunt Letters." *Notes and Queries* n.s. 2 (March 1955):123-24.

1956
"The Chronology of Carey Imprints." *Papers of the Bibliographical Society of America* 50 (1956):190-93.

"The Coordination of Faculty Services," with John C. Abbott. *College & Research Libraries* 17 (January 1956):13-15.

"Home Use of Microfilm." *Library Journal* 81 (June 15, 1956):1606.

"Messrs. Carey and Lea of Philadelphia; 1822-1838." Ph.D. diss., University of Michigan, 1956.

"The Origin of the Book Trade Sales." *Papers of the Bibliographic Society of America* 50 (1956):296-302.

"The Retirement Income of Mathew Carey." *Pennsylvania Magazine of History and Biography* 70 (1956):410-15.

"Twenty-Six Brief Lectures on the History of Printing." *Wilson Library Bulletin* 30 (January 1956):398. Reprinted in *University of Michigan, Department of Library Science, Alumni Notes* 10 (May 1956):29; *Nederlandse Antiquariaat* 10 (July 15, 1958):2-3; *Antiquarian Bookman* 23 (May 11, 1959):1662; Spartanburg, S.C.: Kitemaug Press, 1974; Los Angeles: privately printed, 1982.

"William Warner Bishop: Contributions to a Bibliography." *Library Quarterly* 26 (January 1956):52-60.

1957
"Leigh Hunt and His Pennsylvania Editor." *Pennsylvania Magazine of History and Biography* 81 (1957):406-14.

Messrs. Carey and Lea of Philadelphia; A Study in the History of the Booktrade. Philadelphia: University of Pennsylvania Press, 1957.

"Waverly in America." *Papers of the Bibliographical Society of America* 51 (1957):163-67.

1958
"Authur L. Kaser: Gag Man for the Amateur." *Books at Brown* 18 (1958):94-115.

"Discounts and Service." *Missouri Library Association Quarterly* 19 (1958):92-95.

"The First Trans-Mississippi Imprint." *Papers of the Bibliographical Society of America* 52 (1958):306-9.

Washington University Manuscripts: A Descriptive Guide, with Jane Kaser. St. Louis: Washington University Libraries, 1958.

1959
"Division Reports: Resources and Technical Services Division; Serials Section." *Library Journal* 84 (July 1959):2147.

"Editorial." *Missouri Library Association Quarterly* 20 (1959):32, 64, 96, 122.

Report on a Grant. *American Philosophical Society Yearbook* (1959):562-63.

1960
"Editorial." *Missouri Library Association Quarterly* 21 (1960):48.

"The Literature of Acquisitions." In *The Literature of Library Technical Services*, 7-12. University of Illinois Library School, Occasional Papers, no. 58. Urbana, 1960.

"1959—Bumper Year for Serials." *Library Resources & Technical Services* 4 (1960):125-28.

1961
"About *A Directory of the St. Louis Book and Printing Trades to 1850.*" *New York Public Library Bulletin* 65 (November 1961):583-87.

"The Booktrade and Publishing History." In *Research Opportunities in American Cultural History*, edited by John Francis McDermott, 140-54. Lexington: University of Kentucky Press, 1961.

A Directory of the St. Louis Book and Printing Trades to 1850. New York: New York Public Library, 1961.

"How Big Is a Research Library?" *Peabody Reflector* 34 (1961):117-19.

"The Interdependence of Academic Libraries." *Kentucky Library Association Bulletin* 25 (April 1961):3-9.

Report on a Grant. *American Philosophical Society Yearbook* (1961):526-28.

"The Year's Work in Serials." *Library Resources & Technical Services* 5 (1961):129-34.

1962
"Automation in Libraries of the Future." *Tennessee Librarian* 14 (1962):79-84.

"In Principio Erat Verbum." *Peabody Journal of Education* 39 (1962):258-63.

"The Joint University Libraries." In *College and University Interinstitutional Cooperation*, edited by J. J. Wittich, 50-51. Corning, N.Y.: College Center of the Finger Lakes, 1962.

"Joint University Libraries Big Enough to Overwhelm Aristotle." *Nashville Tennessean* (April 29, 1962):9-ED.

"Serial Activities in 1961." *Library Resources & Technical Services* 6 (1962): 135-42.

1963
"The Arlie Conference." *College & Research Libraries* 24 (1963):337-38.

The Cost Book of Carey and Lea, 1825-1838, edited by David Kaser. Philadelphia: University of Pennsylvania Press, 1963.

"Dr. Kaser Discusses the Young University Library." *Mississippi Library News* 27 (1963):144-46.

"Eighth Midwest Academic Librarians Conference." *College & Research Libraries* 24 (1963):334.

Joseph Charless, Printer in the Western Country. Philadelphia: University of Pennsylvania Press, 1963.

"The Library and the Graduate School." *Council of Graduate Schools in the United States, Proceedings* 3 (1963):202-10.

"The Literature of Acquisitions." In *The Literature of Library Technical Services*, 7-13. Rev. ed. University of Illinois Library School, Occasional Papers, no. 58. Urbana, 1963.

"Outside Funding of Academic Libraries." *Library Trends* 11 (1963):353-61.

"Serial Activities in 1962." *Library Resources & Technical Services* 7 (1963): 169-75.

1964

"The Library in the Young University." *Southeastern Librarian* 14 (1964):174-80.

"Library School Libraries." *Journal of Education for Librarianship* 5 (1964): 17-19.

"Nashville's Women of Pleasure in 1860." *Tennessee Historical Quarterly* 23 (1964):379-82.

"Professionalism in an Age of Change." *Kentucky Library Association Bulletin* 28 (1964):6-14. Reprinted in *Southeastern Librarian* 14 (1964):42-47; *Library Occurrent* 21 (1964):127-31.

"Science, Industry, and the Research Library." In *Twentieth Biennial Conference, Southwestern Library Association, October 21-24, 1964. Papers and Proceedings*, 72-79. Little Rock, Ark., 1964.

1965

"Acquisitions Work in the Next Twenty Years." *Southeastern Librarian* 15 (1965):90-94

"Binders on the American Frontier." *Rub-Off* 16 (May-June 1965):2-4.

"The Golden Touch; or the Gentle Art of Raising Money." *Stechert-Hafner Book News* 19 (1965):109-11.

"The Library in the Small Historical Society." *American Association for State and Local History, Technical Leaflet*, no. 27 (*History News* v. 20, no. 4, April 1965).

"Science, Industry, and the Library." *Arkansas Libraries* 21 (1965):21-28.

1966

"Academic Science and the University Library." *University of Tennessee Library Lectures* 17 (1966):8-20.

"Bernard Dornin, America's First Catholic Bookseller." In *Books in America's Past*, edited by David Kaser, 105-28. Charlottesville: University Press of Virginia, 1966.

Books in America's Past: Essays Honoring Rudolph H. Gjelsness, edited by David Kaser. Charlottesville: University Press of Virginia, 1966.

Developmental Book Activities and Needs in the Republic of Korea, with S. A. Barnett, E. D. Michener, and C. W. Stone. Washington, D.C.: Agency for International Development, 1966.

A Directory of the Book and Printing Industries in Ante-Bellum Nashville. New York: New York Public Library, 1966.

"Eleventh Annual Midwest Academic Librarians Conference." *ACRL News* 4 (June 1966):69-70.

"Introduction to *A Directory of the Book and Printing Industries in Ante-Bellum Nashville.*" *New York Public Library Bulletin* 70 (April 1966):209-17.

"Korean Micro-Libraries and Private Reading Rooms." *Library Journal* 91 (1966):6035-38.

1967
"Academic Science and the University Library." In *The Library in the University*, 276-88. Hamden, Conn.: Shoe String Press, 1967.

"College Libraries in Tennessee." *Tennessee Librarian* 20 (1967):59-63.

"Continuing Education in the Library Profession." In *Louisiana State University Library Lectures*, 1-9. Baton Rouge: Louisiana State University, 1966.

Developmental Book Activities and Needs in Laos, with S. A. Barnett and E. Brown. Washington, D.C.: Agency for International Development, 1967.

"Dispelling Hunches, Intuition, and That Professional Mystique." *Wilson Library Bulletin* 41 (May 1967):923-25.

"Famine in a Land of Plenty." *Southeastern Librarian* 17 (1967):74-80.

"Research Libraries in the National Interest." *Vanderbilt Alumnus* 52 (January-February 1967):11-14.

1968
"Korea: Herculean Effort in the Land of the Morning Calm." *Library Journal* 93 (November 15, 1968):4251-54.

"Tom Brown's Library at Rugby." In *Proceedings of the Third Library History Seminar*, edited by M. J. K. Zachert, 124-36. Tallahassee, Journal of Library History, 1968.

1969
"The Academic Librarian and Protocol of Scholarship." *Library Journal* 94 (February 15, 1969):719-21.

Book Pirating in Taiwan. Philadelphia: University of Pennsylvania Press, 1969. Reprinted, Taipei: Mei Ya, 1969.

"Books and Libraries in the Far East." *Wilson Library Bulletin* 43 (June 1969):974-79.

"The Dynamics of Library Development." *Rice University Studies* 55 (Fall 1969):37-43.

Library Development in Eight Asian Countries, with C. W. Stone and C. K. Byrd. Metuchen, N.J.: Scarecrow, 1969. Translated as *Pal chyun tosang kuk il t'osogwan*. Seoul: Korean Library Association, 1970.

"Library Development in the Republic of China." *National Taiwan University Library Science Circular*, no. 14 (May 1969):1-14.

"Problems in International Librarianship." *National Taiwan University Library Science Circular*, no. 18 (November 1969):1-7. Reprinted in *Library Progress* 3 (1970):77-82.

1970

"David Kaser." In *The Librarian Speaking*, edited by G. R. Lyle, 57-70. Athens: University of Georgia Press, 1970.

"Extra-Library Barriers to Interlibrary Cooperation." In *Rationalizing Research Libraries in the 70's*, 33-38. Syracuse: Five Associated University Libraries, 1970.

"Junior College Libraries In Tennessee," with Ken Yamada. *Tennessee Librarian* 22 (Spring 1970):117-21.

"Modernizing the University Library Structure." *College & Research Libraries* 31 (July 1970):227-31.

"Museums, Toolrooms, and Arsenals." *Libraries in International Development*, no. 23 (June 1970):1-2.

"Reader's Report." *John M. Olin Library Bookmark*, no. 43, April 1970.

"Report of the Director of the Cornell University Libraries: 1969-70." *AB Bookman's Weekly* 46 (December 14, 1970):1827-32.

"Staff Role in Goal Determination." In *Papers Delivered at the Indiana University Library Dedication, October 9-10, 1970*, 64-68. Bloomington, Ind., 1970.

"Wisdom and Knowledge in Consortium Building." *Bookmark* 29 (March 1970):221-25.

1971

"Books for International Studies." *Cornell University International Studies Bulletin* 2 (May 1971):1-2; Alumni Issue, 1971:2-3.

"Cornell Collection Development." *AB Bookman's Weekly* 48 (December 20-27, 1971):2003.

"FAUL: A Consortium Approach to Library Automation." In *Collaborative Library Systems Development*, edited by P. J. Fasana and A. Veaner, 106-9. Cambridge: MIT Press, 1971.

"Making the Effort." In *New Directions in Staff Development*, edited by E. W. Stone, 6-10. Chicago: American Library Association, 1971.

"Organizing an Oriental Collection." *Foreign Acquisitions Newsletter*, no. 33 (Spring 1971):2-5.

"Planning in University Libraries: Context and Processes." *Southeastern Librarian* 21 (Winter 1971):207-13.

"The Ptolemaic Theory of Librarianship." *Oklahoma Librarian* 21 (July 1971):10-13.

"The Training Subsystem." *Library Trends* 20 (July 1971):71-77.

1972
"Funk, Isaac Kauffman." *Encyclopedia Americana* (1972), XII:178.

"Gannett, Frank Ernest." *Encyclopedia Americana* (1972), XII:286.

"Library Development in Asia." *Encyclopedia Americana* (1972), XVII:324-36.

"Preface." In *A. Hart, Philadelphia Publisher, (1829-1854)*, by Louis Ginsberg, i-ii. Petersburg, Va.: The Author, 1972.

"The United States Book Industry Abroad." *Library Trends* 20 (January 1972):500-505.

"Whither Interlibrary Loan?" *College & Research Libraries* 33 (September 1972):398-402.

1973
Report by New York State, Education Department, Advisory Committee on Planning for the Academic Libraries, 1-12, 25-31. Albany, N.Y.: Education Department, 1973.

1974
"A Dialectic for Planning in Academic Libraries." In *Academic Libraries*, edited by E. I. Farber, 96-104. Metuchen, N.J.: Scarecrow Press, 1974.

"Evaluation of Administrative Services." *Library Trends* 22 (January 1974):257-64.

"Library Access and the Mobility of Users." *College & Research Libraries* 35 (July 1974):280-84.

1975
"Humanism, the Library, and the Quality of Life." *Journal of Library and Information Science* 1 (October 1975):25-35.

"Standards for College Libraries," with the ACRL Ad Hoc Committee to Revise the 1959 Standards. *College & Research Libraries News* 36 (October 1975):277-79, 290-95, 298-301.

1976
"A Century of Academic Librarianship as Reflected in Its Literature." *College & Research Libraries* 37 (March 1976):110-27.

"A Century of Personnel Concerns in Libraries," with Ruth Jackson. In *A Century of Service*, 129-45. Chicago: American Library Association, 1976.

"President's Report." *Beta Phi Mu Newsletter*, no. 39 (March 1976):1-3.

1977
"A Century of Academic Librarianship, as Reflected in Its Literature." In *Libraries for Teaching; Libraries for Research*, edited by R. D. Johnson, 219-36. Chicago: American Library Association, 1977.

"The Effect of the Revolution of 1969-1970 on University Library Administration." In *Academic Libraries by the Year 2000; Essays Honoring Jerrold Orne*, edited by H. Poole, 64-75. New York: Bowker, 1977.

"International Organizations." In *Recent Developments in Comparative and International Library Science*, edited by J. F. Harvey, 39-47. Metuchen, N.J.: Scarecrow Press, 1977.

The Viability of Merging Three Academic Libraries in Worcester, with Jinnie Y. Davis. Bloomington, Ind.: Indiana University Graduate Library School, 1977.

1978
"Advances in American Library History." In *Advances in Librarianship,* vol. 8, edited by M. H. Harris, 181-99. New York: Academic Press, 1978.

"Coffee House to Stock Exchange: A Natural History of the Reading Room." In *Milestones to the Present*, edited by H. Goldstein, 238-54. Syracuse: Gaylord Professional Publications, 1978.

"Eileen Roach Cunningham." In *Dictionary of American Library Biography*, 107-8. Littleton, Colo.: Libraries Unlimited, 1978.

"The Library Mission in the Academic Environment." In *Objective Setting for Illinois Libraries*, edited by P. Breivik, 28-32. Springfield: Illinois Library Association, 1978.

"Randolph Greenfield Adams." In *Dictionary of American Library Biography*, 2-3. Littleton, Colo.: Libraries Unlimited, 1978.

"Toward a Conceptual Foundation for a National Information Policy." *Wilson Library Bulletin* 52 (1978): 545-49.

1979
"Toward a Conceptual Foundation for a National Information Policy." In *Library Lit. 9—The Best of 1978*, edited by B. Katz, 128-35. Metuchen, N.J.: Scarecrow Press, 1979.

"Tuei le! Tang jan yao t'u shu kuan." *Bulletin of the Library Association of China* 31 (December 2, 1979):110-12.

1980
A Book for a Sixpence; The Circulating Library in America. Pittsburgh: Beta Phi Mu, 1980.

"Carey and Lea." In *Publishers for Mass Entertainment in Nineteenth Century America*, edited by M. B. Stern, 73-80. Boston: G. K. Hall, 1980.

"Collection Building in American Universities." In *University Library History*, edited by J. Thompson, 33-55. New York: Clive Bingley, 1980.

"Kilgour, Frederick Gridley." In *ALA World Encyclopedia of Library and Information Science*, 290-91. Chicago: American Library Association, 1980.

"Lemuel Blake and William Pynson Blake." In *Boston Printers, Publishers, and Booksellers: 1640-1800*, edited by Benjamin Franklin V, 34-41. Boston: G. K. Hall, 1980.

"Metcalf, Keyes Dewitt." In *ALA World Encyclopedia of Library and Information Science*, 367-68. Chicago: American Library Association, 1980.

"Planning Library Service." In *Library Planning and Media Technology*, 18-100. Taipei: Library Association of China, 1980.

"Significance of Libraries: Four Cases." *Journal of Library and Information Science* 6 (October 1980):131-39.

"Why Libraries Indeed?" *Republic of China National Central Library Newsletter* 11 (January 1980):86-91.

1981
"American Academic Library Architecture, 1840-1980." In *Metcalf, Downs, Kaser, and Shera*, 20-28. *Library Journal*, Special Report, no. 21.

"Prof. Abdul Moid." In *Dr. Moid and Pakistani Librarianship*, 13-14. Karachi: Library Promotion Bureau, 1981.

1982
"Examining Education Frontiers." *ASIS Bulletin* 8 (April 1982):30.

"Significance, Method, and Creativity in Library Research." In *University of North Carolina, School of Library Science, Fiftieth Anniversary*, 1-11. Bookmark, 51-52, 1982.

"Standards for College Libraries." *Library Trends* 31 (Summer 1982):7-19.

"Ying chieh erh-shih-i shih chi te t'u shu kuan" (The Library of the 21st Century). *Library Association of China Newsletter*, no. 30 (July 15, 1982):9-12.

1983
"The Dewey Era in American Librarianship." In *Melvil Dewey: The Man and the Classification*, edited by G. Stevenson, 9-24. Albany, N.Y.: Forest Press, 1983.

"Dix, William Shepherd." In *Encyclopedia of Library and Information Science*, vol. 36, 182-86. New York: Marcel Dekker, 1983.

"Foreword." In *Ten Years Work in Librarianship in Pakistan 1973-1982*, i-ii. Karachi: Mahmood Khan, 1983.

"Free Knowledge or Fettered Minds?" *Journal of Library and Information Science* 9 (April 1983):19-26.

1984
Books and Libraries in Camp and Battle: The Civil War Experience. Westport, Conn.: Greenwood, 1984.

"Twenty-Five Years of Academic Library Building Planning." *College & Research Libraries* 45 (July 1984):268-81.

1985
"The Role of the Building in the Delivery of Library Service." In *Access to Scholarly Information*, edited by S. H. Lee, 13-24. Ann Arbor, Mich.: Pierian Press, 1985.

1986
"The American Academic Library Building, 1870-1890." *Journal of Library History* 21 (Winter 1986):60-71.

"Library Buildings." In *ALA World Encyclopedia of Library and Information Science*, 2d ed., 467-71. Chicago: American Library Association, 1986.

"Planning Library Buildings in Other Lands." In *Planning Library Buildings from Decision to Design*, edited by L. K. Smith, 189-91. Chicago: American Library Association, 1986.

1987
"Designing New Space: Some Old Realities." *Library Hi Tech* 5 (Winter 1987):87-89.

"Interview with David Kaser." *Library Administration & Management* 1 (June 1987):76-77.

"19th-Century Academic Library Buildings." *College & Research Libraries News* 48 (September 1987):476-78.

"The Sinking of the *ALA*," *Library Journal* 112 (June 1, 1987):74-77.

"Dewey Centennial Rap." *LHRT Newsletter* (Fall 1987):4.

1988
"Academic Library Buildings: Their Evolution and Prospects." In *Advances in Library Administration and Organization*, vol. 7, 149-60. Greenwich, Conn.: JAI Press, 1988.

"Joseph Charless." In *Lexikon des gesamten Buchwesens*, 2d ed., 96. Stuttgart: Anton Hiersemann, 1988.

"Richard Barksdale Harwell." *Proceedings of the American Antiquarian Society* 98, pt. 1 (1988):28-29.

Appendix C
Doctoral Students Supervised by David Kaser

Michael Afolabi, "The Literature of Bibliographical Classification: A Citation Study to Determine the Core Literature," Ph.D. dissertation, Indiana University, 1983. 204pp.

Yahya Assadi, "An Investigation for a Model for Extending Library Services to Rural Areas in Iran," Ph.D. dissertation, Indiana University, 1977. 236pp.

Abdulrasheed A. Attalrahman, "Resource Sharing and Information Networking among University Libraries in Saudi Arabia," Ph.D. dissertation, Indiana University, 1977. 236pp.

Earl Bean, "Response Rates to Questionnaires Used in Library Science and in Selected Cognate Disciplines as Reported in Scholarly Periodicals," Ph.D. dissertation, Indiana University, in progress.

Nassir Bello, "The 1970 Library Decree of the Federal Military Government of Nigeria, and Its Impact on the Functions, Development, and Extension of the National Library," Ph.D. dissertation, Indiana University, 1982. 259pp.

William A. Caynon Jr., "A Study of the Relationship Between Collective Bargaining Environments and the Professional Development Activities of Academic Librarians," Ph.D. dissertation, Indiana University, 1980. 254pp.

Robert Chen, "Library Resources for American Studies in Taiwan: An Evaluation," Ph.D. dissertation, Indiana University, 1976. 151pp.

Evelyn Clement, "Audiovisual Concerns and Activities of the American Library Association, 1924-1975," Ph.D. dissertation, Indiana University, 1975. 171pp.

Reginald P. Coady, "The Applicability of Markov Models to the Circulation of Social-Science Monographs in a Large Academic Library," Ph.D. dissertation, Indiana University, 1981. 120pp.

William J. Crowe, "Verner W. Clapp as Opinion Leader and Change Agent in the Preservation of Library Materials," Ph.D. dissertation, Indiana University, 1986. 151pp.

Jinnie Y. Davis, "Individuals, Information, and Structure in the Establishment of OCLC: A Study of Innovation Decision Making," Ph.D. dissertation, Indiana University, 1980. 344pp.

Margaret C. Fung, "The Evolving Social Mission of the National Central Library in China, 1928-1966," Ph.D. dissertation, Indiana University, 1983. 406pp.

Bruce G. Golden, "A Study of the Relationship Between Selected Community College Instructors' Utilization of the Learning Resources Materials and Student Ratings of Teaching Effectiveness," Ph.D. dissertation, Indiana University, 1981. 130pp.

Pensi Guaysuwan, "The Impact of the Indiana University-Thailand Contract in Teacher Education on the Development of Library Resources and Services in Thailand," Ph.D. dissertation, Indiana University, 1985. 307pp.

Charles E. Hale, "The Origin and Development of the Association of College and Research Libraries, 1889-1960," Ph.D. dissertation, Indiana University, 1976. 294pp.

Larry L. Hardesty, "The Development of a Set of Scales to Measure the Attitudes of Classroom Instructors Toward the Undergraduate Educational Role of the Academic Library," Ph.D. dissertation, Indiana University, 1982. 370pp.

Epsy Y. Hendricks, "The Role of Personnel Officers in University Libraries," Ph.D. dissertation, Indiana University, 1977. 306pp.

Betty Jo Irvine, "Female and Male Administrators in Academic Research Libraries: Individual and Institutional Variables Influencing the Attainment of Top Administrative Positions," Ph.D. dissertation, Indiana University, 1982. 287pp.

Ruth L. Moore Jackson, "Origin and Development of Selected Personnel Management Functions in the Field of American Librarianship, 1876-1969," Ph.D. dissertation, Indiana University, 1976. 565pp.

Abulfazal M. Fazle Kabir, "Origin and Growth of Libraries in Bengal from 1700 Through British Rule, 1757-1947," Ph.D. dissertation, Indiana University, 1982. 302pp.

Barbara Kasper, "A Comparative Analysis of Public Library Service to Children in Indiana during the 1970s," Ph.D. dissertation, Indiana University, 1985. 176pp.

Ung Chou Kim, "A Statistical Study of Factors Affecting Salaries of Academic Librarians at Medium-Sized State-Supported Universities in Five Midwestern States," Ph.D. dissertation, Indiana University, 1980. 193pp.

James Kusack, "Support Staff Unions in University Libraries in the United States: A Description and Analysis of Selected Characteristics," Ph.D. dissertation, Indiana University, 1984. 169pp.

Darryl H. Lemke, "Origins, Structures, and Activities of Five Academic Library Consortia," Ph.D. dissertation, Indiana University, 1975. 324pp.

Jannith L. Lewis, "Strategies for Attaining Quantitative Adequacy in the Collections of Selected Undergraduate Liberal Arts College Libraries Evaluated by College Library Standards," Ph.D. dissertation, Indiana University, 1982. 142pp.

Wilson C. Luquire, "Selected Factors Affecting Library Staff Perceptions of an Innovative System: A Study of ARL Libraries in OCLC," Ph.D. dissertation, Indiana University, 1976. 127pp.

Jean A. Major, "The Effect of Search Dialogue in an On-Line Subject Catalog: An Experimental Study of Four Feedback Mechanisms," Ph.D. dissertation, Indiana University, 1981. 97pp.

Judith Mowery, "Correlates of Professionalism among Academic Librarians," Ph.D. dissertation, Indiana University, 1986. 316pp.

James L. Mullins, "A Study of Selected Factors Affecting Growth Rates of American Law School Libraries," Ph.D. dissertation, Indiana University, 1984. 100pp.

Richard Newman, "The Public's Right to Government Information: An Examination of Press Use of the Freedom of Information Act to Gain Information about the U.S. Foreign Intelligence Agencies," Ph.D. dissertation, Indiana University, in progress.

Naila Nshaiwat, "Fee-Based Information Service Managers in Academic Libraries: Some Entrepreneurial Characteristics," Ph.D. dissertation, Indiana University, in progress.

Joanne E. Passet, "Quest for a Profession: The Origins of Library Education in Indiana," Ph.D. dissertation, Indiana University, 1988. 227pp.

John V. Richardson Jr., "The Spirit of Inquiry in Library Science: The Graduate Library School at Chicago, 1921-1951," Ph.D. dissertation, Indiana University, 1978. 437pp.

Nancy P. Sanders, "Some Factors for Predicting Changes in Library Support from the University During Periods of Economic Decline," Ph.D. dissertation, Indiana University, 1982. 150pp.

Mohamed M. Sibai, "An Historical Investigation of Mosque Libraries in Islamic Life and Culture," Ph.D. dissertation, Indiana University, 1984. 447pp.

Aime S. Thoumy, "University Publishing in Lebanon: A Historical and Comparative Study of the Publishing Programs of the Five Universities in Lebanon," Ph.D. dissertation, Indiana University, 1981. 175pp.

Michael Waldo, "A Comparative Analysis of Nineteenth-Century Academic and Literary Society Library Collections in the Midwest," Ph.D. dissertation, Indiana University, 1985. 226pp.

Mei-Hwa Yang, "Library Education and Personnel Planning in the Republic of China," Ph.D. dissertation, Indiana University, 1986. 158pp.

Appendix D
Building and Space Consultancies of David Kaser

Name of Library	Gross Sq. Ft.	Nature of Work
1958		
Washington University St. Louis, Missouri	180,000	Assistant Director of Libraries
1962		
Union College Barbourville, Kentucky	20,000	Consultant to owner Program only
1963		
Morristown College Morristown, Tennessee	3,000	Consultant to owner Two days only
1964		
Northeast Missouri State University Kirksville, Missouri	102,000	Consultant to owner Program only
Kansas Wesleyan University Salina, Kansas	55,600	Consultant to owner Program only
1965		
Little Rock University Little Rock, Arkansas	150,000	Consultant to owner
1966		
Carson-Newman College Jefferson City, Tennessee	75,000	Consultant to owner
John F. Kennedy College Wahoo, Nebraska	37,000	Consultant to owner Program only
Hendrix College Conway, Arkansas	30,600	Consultant to owner

Name of Library	Gross Sq. Ft.	Nature of Work
1967		
Alabama A & M University Huntsville, Alabama	60,000	Consultant to owner Program only
University of Montevallo Montevallo, Alabama	52,400	Consultant to owner Program only
1968		
David Lipscomb College Nashville, Tennessee	60,000	Consultant to architect
Tennessee Eastman Company Kingsport, Tennessee	10,000	Consultant to architect
Scarritt College Nashville, Tennessee	38,700	Director of Libraries
Delta State University Cleveland, Mississippi	54,800	Consultant to owner
Emory and Henry College Emory, Virginia	41,932	Consultant to owner Two days only
Memphis State University Memphis, Tennessee	130,000	Consultant to owner Two days only
1969		
Roger Williams College Providence, Rhode Island	30,000	Consultant to owner Program only
Benedict College Columbia, South Carolina	71,800	Consultant to owner
State University of New York College Brockport, New York	150,000	Consultant to architect
University of South Carolina Columbia, South Carolina	n.a.	Consultant to owner Options review
Virginia Wesleyan College Norfolk, Virginia	50,000	Consultant to owner Two days only
Emory University Atlanta, Georgia	240,000	Consultant to owner Two days only

Wofford College Spartanburg, South Carolina	43,000	Consultant to owner
Vanderbilt University Nashville, Tennessee	183,000	Director of Libraries Expansion
1970 Vanderbilt University Science Library Nashville, Tennessee	33,000	Director of Libraries
1971 University of Wisconsin Green Bay, Wisconsin	175,000	Consultant to owner
St. Francis College Fort Wayne, Indiana	50,500	Consultant to owner Program only
University of North Carolina Charlotte, North Carolina	140,000	Consultant to architect
Community College of Finger Lakes Canandaigua, New York	18,000	Consultant to architect
1972 Alfred University Alfred, New York	70,000	Consultant to owner Program only
Cornell University Art Library Ithaca, New York	n.a.	Director of Libraries Program only
1974 Vassar College Poughkeepsie, New York	36,600	Consultant to owner Expansion
East Carolina University Greenville, North Carolina	92,500	Consultant to owner Expansion
1975 Western Illinois University Macomb, Illinois	240,000	Consultant to architect
King Saud University Riyadh, Saudi Arabia	749,000	Consultant to architect
St. Mary's College Notre Dame, Indiana	80,000	Consultant to owner

Name of Library	Gross Sq. Ft.	Nature of Work
1976		
King Abdulaziz Military Academy Riyadh, Saudi Arabia	81,400	Consultant to architect
Lehigh University Bethlehem, Pennsylvania	60,000	Consultant to owner Expansion
1977		
Case Western Reserve University Cleveland, Ohio	n.a.	Consultant to owner Expansion
Bayero University Kano, Nigeria	180,000	Consultant to owner Program only
1978		
Hassanuddin University Ujung Pandang, Indonesia	110,000	Consultant to owner Program only
Western Carolina University Cullowhee, North Carolina	160,000	Consultant to owner Expansion
1979		
St. Meinrad College St. Meinrad, Indiana	45,000	Consultant to owner
Westminster College New Wilmington, Pennsylvania	n.a.	Consultant to owner Options review
University of Oklahoma Norman, Oklahoma	150,000	Consultant to owner Expansion
College of St. Scholastica Duluth, Minnesota	38,000	Consultant to owner Expansion
1980		
Seton Hall University South Orange, New Jersey	n.a.	Consultant to owner Options review
George Mason University Fairfax, Virginia	n.a.	Consultant to owner Options review
University of Evansville Evansville, Indiana	83,000	Consultant to owner Expansion
Bethel College Mishawaka, Indiana	20,000	Consultant to owner

New Brunswick Seminary New Brunswick, New Jersey	n.a.	Consultant to owner Options review

1981

Lee College Cleveland, Tennessee	60,000	Consultant to owner
Illinois Wesleyan University Bloomington, Illinois	n.a.	Consultant to owner Options review
Ewha Women's University Seoul, Korea	213,000	Consultant to owner
Rutgers University Art Library New Brunswick, New Jersey	18,800	Consultant to owner Expansion
Indiana State University Evansville, Indiana	n.a.	Consultant to owner Expansion
Bucknell University Lewisburg, Pennsylvania	147,000	Consultant to owner Expansion

1982

National Institute of the Arts Taipei, Taiwan	61,000	Consultant to owner Program only
Muslim Students Association Plainsfield, Indiana	11,800	Consultant to owner Layout only
Rollins College Winter Park, Florida	54,000	Consultant to owner

1983

University of Petroleum Dhahran, Saudi Arabia	142,000	Consultant to owner Expansion
University of Alberta Edmonton, Alberta, Canada	n.a.	Consultant to owner Options review
Florida Atlantic University Boca Raton, Florida	165,000	Consultant to architect Expansion
Wichita State University Wichita, Kansas	190,000	Consultant to architect Expansion
College of St. Benedict St. Joseph, Minnesota	51,000	Consultant to owner

Name of Library	Gross Sq. Ft.	Nature of Work
Hope College Holland, Michigan	n.a.	Consultant to owner Options review
Lafayette College Easton, Pennsylvania	70,000	Consultant to owner
Taylor University Upland, Indiana	60,000	Consultant to owner
Southwestern University Georgetown, Texas	66,000	Consultant to owner
Western Evangelical Seminary Portland, Oregon	n.a.	Consultant to owner
Huntington College Huntington, Indiana	40,500	Consultant to owner
Rutgers University New Brunswick, New Jersey	n.a.	Consultant to owner Options review
Wabash College Crawfordsville, Indiana	60,000	Consultant to owner Expansion

1984

Name of Library	Gross Sq. Ft.	Nature of Work
New York City Technical College Brooklyn, New York	45,000	Consultant to architect
Transylvania University Lexington, Kentucky	35,300	Consultant to owner Expansion
DePauw University Greencastle, Indiana	52,300	Consultant to owner Renovation
Bellarmine College Louisville, Kentucky	52,800	Consultant to owner
Northern Kentucky University Highland Heights, Kentucky	n.a.	Consultant to owner Options review
Saginaw Valley St. College University Center, Michigan	51,500	Consultant to architect
College of Wooster Wooster, Ohio	n.a.	Consultant to owner Options review
Mary Washington College Fredericksburg, Virginia	n.a.	Consultant to owner Options review

Rhodes College Memphis, Tennessee	n.a.	Consultant to owner Renovation
1985 Maryville College Maryville, Tennessee	35,400	Consultant to owner
Augustana College Rock Island, Illinois	76,500	Consultant to owner
La Salle University Philadelphia, Pennsylvania	113,500	Consultant to owner
Alderson-Broaddus College Philippi, West Virginia	35,000	Consultant to owner Renovation
Kentucky State University Frankfort, Kentucky	n.a.	Consultant to owner Options review
College of Mt. St. Joseph Mount St. Joseph, Ohio	n.a.	Consultant to owner Renovation
1986 Hahnemann University Philadelphia, Pennsylvania	44,400	Consultant to owner Expansion
Whitworth College Spokane, Washington	n.a.	Consultant to owner Options review
Monmouth College West Long Branch, New Jersey	n.a.	Consultant to owner Options review
Western Michigan University Kalamazoo, Michigan	n.a.	Consultant to owner Expansion
Sterling College Sterling, Kansas	22,430	Consultant to owner Options review
Shawnee State University Portsmouth, Ohio	69,300	Consultant to architect
Cincinnati Historical Society Cincinnati, Ohio	n.a.	Consultant to owner
Anderson College Anderson, Indiana	n.a.	Consultant to architect Renovation

Name of Library	Gross Sq. Ft.	Nature of Work
Centre College Danville, Kentucky	67,570	Consultant to architect Renovation
1987 Florida A & M University Tallahassee, Florida	80,000	Consultant to architect
Kent State University Kent, Ohio	n.a.	Consultant to owner Renovation
Olivet College Olivet, Michigan	36,700	Consultant to owner
Bard College Annandale-on-Hudson, New York	n.a.	Consultant to owner Options review
Philadelphia College of Textiles Philadelphia, Pennsylvania	43,000	Consultant to owner
Hampton University Hampton, Virginia	n.a.	Consultant to owner
Stetson University DeLand, Florida	98,400	Consultant to owner Options review
Norfolk State University Norfolk, Virginia	129,000	Consultant to architect
Mankato State University Mankato, Minnesota	176,170	Consultant to architect Expansion
Florida A & M University Tallahassee, Florida	80,000	Consultant to architect Expansion
Olivet College Olivet, Michigan	36,570	Consultant to owner Expansion
Kent State University Kent, Ohio	n.a.	Consultant to owner Options review
Bard College Annandale-on-Hudson, New York	44,600	Consultant to owner Expansion
Philadelphia College of Textiles Philadelphia, Pennsylvania	39,280	Consultant to owner Expansion

Hampton University Hampton, Virginia	n.a.	Consultant to owner Options review
Christendom College Front Royal, Virginia	6,700	Consultant to owner Expansion
J.P. Getty Center Santa Monica, California	n.a.	Consultant to owner Concept review
Hood College Frederick, Maryland	50,000	Consultant to owner
University of West Florida Pensacola, Florida	153,210	Consultant to owner Expansion

1988

Science Library Ohio State University Columbus, Ohio	n.a.	Consultant to architect
Agnes Scott College Decatur, Georgia	n.a.	Consultant to owner
Washington College Chestertown, Maryland	58,000	Consultant to owner Expansion
Elizabethtown College Elizabethtown, Pennsylvania	50,000	Consultant to architect
Berea College Berea, Kentucky	n.a.	Consultant to architect Expansion
University of Minnesota Duluth, Minnesota	n.a.	Consultant to owner Options review
National Taiwan University Taipei, Taiwan	383,000	Consultant to owner
Eastern Illinois University Charleston, Illinois	n.a.	Consultant to owner Expansion
California State University Long Beach, California	n.a.	Consultant to owner Expansion
Sue Bennett College London, Kentucky	12,000	Consultant to owner Expansion

Name of Library	Gross Sq. Ft.	Nature of Work
University of Scranton Scranton, Pennsylvania	70,000	Consultant to architect
Princeton Theological Seminary Princeton, New Jersey	96,000	Consultant to owner Expansion
Gonzaga University Spokane, Washington	114,100	Consultant to architect
Loyola University Chicago, Illinois	59,826	Consultant to owner
Harding University Searcy, Arkansas	56,000	Consultant to owner Expansion
David Lipscomb University Nashville, Tennessee	52,000	Consultant to owner
Wake Forest University Winston-Salem, North Carolina	185,180	Consultant to architect Expansion

Contributors

William J. Crowe is Assistant Director of Libraries for Technical Services at Ohio State University. His chapter is based on a portion of his dissertation, "Verner W. Clapp as Opinion Leader and Change Agent in the Preservation of Library Materials" (1986), for which David Kaser served as chairman of the doctoral committee. Crowe reports that it was primarily Kaser's unfailing personal encouragement and rapid responses to questions (and draft chapters) that helped him see the dissertation through to completion. He describes David Kaser as "the very best of teachers and a model for any aspiring scholar."

Margaret C. Fung is Visiting Professor of Library and Information Science, National Taiwan University, and Research Associate, Fairbank Center for East Asian Research, Harvard University. In her chapter she reviews David Kaser's contributions to international librarianship by recording his contributions to Sino-American librarianship. His professional expertise and scholarship are universally appreciated by the library community at large and by his Chinese colleagues in particular. The author considers it a great privilege to document David Kaser's remarkable achievements in international librarianship.

Warren J. Haas is President of the Council on Library Resources. He has been a professional colleague of David Kaser for many years through overlapping service on the ARL Board of Directors, proximity of administrative assignments (Kaser at Cornell, Haas at Columbia), and commonly held interests in such matters as academic library building design and the professional education of librarians. Haas admires his elder colleague (by ten days) for his enthusiastic and soundly based support for the profession of librarian and the skill with which he has supported the cause of libraries and academic institutions over the years.

Charles E. Hale is Director of Staley Library at Millikin University. In his chapter he presents a revised and abbreviated segment of one chapter of his doctoral dissertation. That dissertation, entitled "The Origin and Development of the Association of College and Research Libraries, 1889-1960," was completed at Indiana University's Graduate Library School in 1976. David Kaser served as chairman of that doctoral committee, and for his wise, patient, and valuable counsel, Hale will ever be grateful. It seems appropriate that two areas of Dr. Kaser's national reputation—library history and academic librarianship—are the focal points of this chapter.

Larry L. Hardesty is Director of Library Services at Eckerd College in St. Petersburg, Florida. He greatly appreciates the opportunity to contribute to the honoring of David Kaser. Hardesty considers it a small return for the wise counsel Kaser provided as chair of his doctoral research committee — counsel that helped him to avoid many of the pitfalls awaiting the neophyte researcher — and for Kaser's infectious optimism and generous gift of time. **Mark Tucker** is Senior Reference Librarian in the Humanities, Social Science and Education Library at Purdue University, proudly representing "that other Indiana" institution of higher learning. He has long regarded David Kaser as an admirable role model in areas of mutual interest, academic librarianship and library history.

Frederick G. Kilgour is Founder Trustee of the Online Computer Library Center (OCLC). He is delighted to have this opportunity of expressing his profound admiration of David Kaser's productive scholarship. In particular, Kaser's histories of publishing and printing have been major contributions. His scholarly studies of individual publishers provide us with an understanding not only of the development of individual publishing houses but also of publishing in its entirety.

Philip D. Leighton is Building Projects Manager in the Stanford University Libraries, and **David C. Weber** holds the Ida M. Green Chair as the Director of University Libraries at Stanford University. While being eager to join in celebration of Kaser's career, the authors note that when an individual has contributed as much as has David Kaser to research librarianship, library management, library history, and academic library building design, it is a special pleasure to contribute in his honor. Yet, at the same time, it is sobering to attempt to address one of the many topics of Kaser's expertise without his collaboration.

James L. Mullins is Director of Library Services, Indiana University, South Bend. He considers David Kaser the epitome of what should be sought in an academic librarian. The commitment to scholarship and learning Kaser exhibits has been a model for many of us. His professional attitude, tempered with concern for those he teaches and directs, is appreciated by all those with whom he comes into contact.

Joanne E. Passet is an Assistant Professor at the Graduate School of Library and Information Science at the University of California, Los Angeles. She welcomes the opportunity to honor her mentor and friend, David Kaser, who gave generously of his time and knowledge as he guided her through the doctoral program at Indiana University. She deeply appreciates his constant encouragement, tireless energy, wide-ranging expertise, and genuine interest in students — he truly made a difference in her life.

Index

"A.L.A. Publications for College and University Libraries" (Keogh), 90
Academic and research librarianship, 12
 collection development, 103-4
 growth, 99, 103
 interlibrary loan, 89
 library use instruction, 97-105
 professional development programs, 3-7
 publishing and publications, 90-91
 regional associations, 88
 role development, 81-84, 93-94
 statistics, 88-89
Academic Library Management Intern Program of CLR, 6
ACRL. *See* Association of College and Research Libraries
Adams, Herbert Baxter, 99
Advanced Study Program of CRL, 4
Akers, Susan G., 116
ALA. *See* American Library Association; Associate, Library Association
ALA Catalog Rules: Author and Title Entries, 116
Albert, Leo, 124
American Association of University Professors, 68
American Council of Learned Societies, 56
American Historical Association, 98
American Libraries, 60
American Library Association (ALA), 131
 and academic librarianship, 81-84
 leadership, 92, 97
 library instruction surveys, 101
 preservation of library materials, 47, 49-52
 publishing and publications, 90, 91(table)
 sectional programs and selected activities, 85, 87-92
 and Sino-American librarianship, 116-17, 124

American Management Association's Center for Planning, 130
American Philosophical Society, 131
American Society for Information Science (ASIS), 120
Amherst College, 83
"Analysis of Publications Issued by the American Library Association, 1907-1957" (Foreman), 90
Andrews, Clement W., 83, 89
Andrew W. Mellon Foundation, 4
Arkansas, 91
ARL. *See* Association of Research Libraries
Armed Forces Librarians of ALA, 124
Arthur D. Little, Inc., 59
Asbestos, 19
Asia Foundation, 131
ASIS. *See* American Society for Information Science
Associate, Library Association (ALA), 70
Association of American Colleges, 68
Association of College and Research Libraries (ACRL), 131. *See also* College Library Section
 faculty status standards, 67-68, 71-77
 library use instruction, 105
Association of Research Libraries (ARL), 6
 preservation of library materials, 49, 59-60
 professional development programs, 8
 statistics, 89
Association of University Teachers, 68
Austen, William, 101
Austin, Willard, 83

Back-of-the-book indexes, 31, 34-35, 37. *See also* Electronic Information Delivery Online System

Ball State Teachers College, 130
Barrow, William J., 45-48
  library binding project, 52-53
  permanent/durable paper research, 49-52, 56-59
Barrow Laboratory, 57-59
Bestor, Arthur E., Jr., 100
Beta Phi Mu, 131
"Bibliographic Bulletin," 90
Bibliographic instruction. *See* Library use instruction
Bibliographic Instruction Section of ACRL, 105
Bibliography of American College Library Administration, 1899-1926 (Plum), 90
Billings, Harold W., 23
Bishop, William Warner, 86, 92, 130
Bodleian Library, 69-77
Bodley, Sir Thomas, 70
Bonta, Bruce D., 21
Book detection systems, 21
Book Pirating in Taiwan (Kaser), 122-23
Books
  classification schemes, 116
  electronic, 31, 32(fig.), 33-37
  indexes, 31, 34-35, 37
  library collection growth, 99
  major methods for locating information in, 37(table)
  and microfilming, 54
  piracy publishing, 122-23
  success rates for locating in libraries, 33, 35-36
  use research, 36-37
  vs. computer technology, 26
"Books and Libraries in the Far East," 124
Books-for-China campaign, 117
"Books for International Studies" (Kaser), 124
Boone Library School, 115
Bostwick, Arthur Elmore, 116
Bowdoin College, 83, 101
Boxer Indemnity Fund, 116
Branscomb, Harvie, 102
Bristol University, 71-75
British Museum, 46
Brockway, Thomas, 56
Brough, Kenneth J., 103
Brown, Charles Harvey, 116
Brown University, 101
Bryant, Douglas, 51
Burma, 131
Butler Library, 19. *See also* Columbia University

California, University of (Berkeley), 17-18
California, University of (Los Angeles), 6, 8, 17, 23
Cambodia, 131
Cambridge University, 69-70
Canada, 38, 86, 131
Captive Nations Week (1982), 120
Carhart, Forrest, 53
Carnegie Corporation, 4, 101
Cataloging for Small Libraries (Hitchler), 116
Cataloging Rules with Explanation and Illustrations (Fellows), 116
CD-ROM technology, 21-22
Center for Research Libraries, 51
Chen-ku Wang, 117, 121
Chia-chun Ju, William, 117
Chiang Ching-kuo, 124
Chiang Fu-tsung, 118
Chia-pi Hsu, 116
Chicago, University of, 7, 59
Chih-ber Kwei, 116
China. *See* Republic of China
China Foundation for Promotion of Education and Culture, 116
Chinese-American Librarians Associations, 119
Chin-shen Hu, 116
Chi-wu Wang, 122
Chung Hwa Book Company, 123
Church, Randolph W., 46-47, 49
Clapp, Verner Warren
  ARL leadership, 51-52
  CLR leadership, 43-46, 55-57
  copyright projects, 59
  education background, 45
  library binding projects, 52-53
  microfilming projects, 53-54
  preservation of library material projects, 45-50, 53-54, 57-58, 60-61
  Sino-American librarianship, 116
Classification Scheme for Chinese and Japanese Books (Kai-ming Chiu), 116
Clemons, Harry, 115
CLR. *See* Council on Library Resources
"College and Library News," 90

Index / 169

College and Reference Library Section, 83, 86, 88-89, 91, 94
College and Reference Library Work Section, 83, 86. *See also* College and Reference Library Section
College and Research Libraries, 121, 131
College Librarians' Roundtable, 86
College librarianship. *See* Academic and research librarianship
College Libraries in the United States; Contributions toward a Bibliography (Williams), 90
College Library Section
  history, 81-92
  on library use instruction, 105
  membership and organizational concerns, 84-86
  programs and selected activities, 87-91
  reference librarians, 86-87
College Library Section of ALA, 82
Columbia University, 14, 19, 99
Columbus and Franklin County (Ohio) Public Library, 36
Committee on a Revised Form of Library Statistics, 88
Committee on a Union List of Serials, 88
Committee on Bibliographic Instruction, 105
Committee on Cooperation in Indexing and Cataloging in College Libraries, 82
Committee on Educational Qualifications and Status of Professional Librarians in Colleges and Universities, 88
Committee on Foreign Periodicals of the War Period, 88
Committee on Organization of the College Library Section, 83-84
Committee on Permanent/Durable Paper, 49-50, 52
Committee on Preservation of Library Materials, 49
Committee on Preservation of Research Library Materials, 51-52, 59
Committee on Printed Cards for Monographic Series, 88
Committee on Production Guidelines for Book Longevity, 60
Committee on Regional Groupings of Libraries, 88
Committee on Research Libraries, 56
Committee on Standardization of Building Needs, 88

Committee on the Orient and Southwest Pacific, 116
Computer technology and library buildings, 13-28
Conference on Permanent/Durable Paper, 48
Conference on Preservation of Materials in New York, 60
Connecticut, 45
Cooperative Research program of CRL, 4
Copyright laws, 59, 70, 122-24
Cornell University, 83, 118, 130
  collection development, 99
  and computer technology, 17, 22
Council on Library Resources (CLR), 60, 130-31
  Clapp's leadership, 43-46, 55-56
  history, 3, 55-56
  institutional programs, 3-7
  library binding projects, 52-53
  on library use instruction, 105-6
  library program summary, 5(table)
  preservation of library materials projects, 52
  professional education, 6-12
  research and advanced study funding, 4, 10-11
Crerar, John, 83, 89
Cultural Planning and Development Program, 120
Cutler, Phyllis, 22
Cutter's Expansive Classification, 116

Dandison, Basil, 123
Decimal Classification for Chinese Books (Jih-chang Ho and Yung-chin Yuan), 116
"Declaration of Independence: A Case Study in Preservation" (Clapp), 60
Denison University, 82
"Deterioration of Book Stock—Causes and Remedies" (CLR project), 47
Dewey, John, 101
Dewey, Melvil, 99
Dewey Decimal Classification and Relative Index, 116
DiFelice, Clara, 68
Dillon, Howard W., 105
Dix, William, 43, 51
Doctoral dissertations, 89

Drexel University, 82
Dudley, Miriam, 104-5

Earlham College, 105
Eastern College Librarians, 88, 91
Eastern Illinois University, 118
Eastern Michigan University, 105
Eaton, Andrew, 130
Edinburgh University, 70
EIDOS. *See* Electronic Information Delivery Online System
Electronic books. *See* Electronic Information Delivery Online System
Electronic Information Delivery Online System (EIDOS), 31, 33-38
  system architecture, 32(fig.)
Electronic publishing, 24. *See also* Electronic Information Delivery Online System
Emerson, Ralph Waldo, 98
Encyclopedia Americana, 124
Ergonomics, 17-18
Erickson, E. Walfred, 103
Evans, Henry, 101
Evans, Luther, 61
"Evolving Social Mission of the National Central Library 1928-1966" (Fung), 118
Ewha Women's University, 131

Faculty status, 67-69, 71-75
"Faculty Status for Academic Librarians: A Review of the Literature" (Werrell & Sullivan), 68
Fang-fu Li, 116
Farber, Evan I., 104-6
Feast of Saint Lawrence, 132
Fellow, Library Association (FLA), 70
Fellows, Jennie D., 116
Fellowship Program of CLR, 4
Feng, Y. T., 19
Feng-chia University (Taichung), 118
Fiber optics, 20
FLA. *See* Fellow, Library Association
Fletcher, W. I., 83-85, 88
Floppy disks, 21
Folger Shakespeare Library, 44
Ford Foundation, 3, 44, 54-55
Foreman, Carolyn, 90
France, 131

Francis, Frank, 46
"Free Knowledge or Fettered Minds" (Kaser speech), 120
Frick, Elizabeth, 105
Fung, Margaret C., 118, 120
Future of the Research Library (Clapp), 56

Gandalf data switch, 25
Gardin, J. C., 31, 33
Garfield, James A., 98
George Peabody College, 117, 130
Germany, 98
Gerould, James Thayer, 89
GI Bill of 1944, 103
Gjelsness, Rudolph, 130
Goodrich, F. L. D., 91
Gould, Charles H., 89
Grant programs, 3-9, 74, 101
Green Library, 18-19. *See also* Stanford University
Guggenheim Fellowships, 122, 131
Gwinn, Nancy E., 106

Haas, Warren J., 59-60
Harris, G. W., 83
Harvard Guide to American History, 131
Harvard University, 51, 97, 101
  collection development, 82, 99
  library automation, 14-15, 19
  Sino-American librarianship, 118
Hazlett, Ray W., 129
Heathcote, Denis, 18
Henry V, 70
Henry VIII, 70
Higham, Norman, 71, 74-75
Hitchler, Theresa, 116
Hollerith punched cards, 14
Hong Kong, 118, 122
Hopkins, Mark, 98-99
Houghton College, 129
"How People Use Books and Journals" (Sabine & Sabine), 36
Hsing-hui Huang, 116
Hsiu Cha, 115
Hsiu-ying Chiang, 119
"Humanism, the Library and Quality of Life" (Kaser), 119
Humphrey, Duke of Gloucester, 70
Hung-tu Tien, 116
Hurt, Peyton, 102
Hutchins, Robert, 101

IBM 1401 computers, 15
IBM keypunch machines, 15
ILL. *See* Interlibrary loan
Illinois, 118-19
"Improvement of Permanence/Durability of Book Papers" (CLR project), 47
Indexes and abstracts, 89
    back-of-the-book indexes, 31, 34-35, 37
    CD-ROM technology, 21-22
    electronic online systems, 31, 32(fig.), 33-37
    online services, 25
Indiana University, 90, 118-20, 131-32
Indiana University Alumni Association, 120
Indonesia, 131
"Information Studies, the Information Professions, and Research Library Leadership" (conference topic), 9-12
Institute for Administrative Officers of Higher Education, 102
Institute of Chinese Architects, 120
Institute of Paper Chemistry, 50, 59
Intelligent buildings, 26-27
Interlibrary loan (ILL), 22, 24, 89, 99
International Conference of Librarians, 97
Internships for recent graduates, 6
"Investigations re: Acidity in Documents" (Barrow), 57
Ireland, 131

Japan, 122, 131
Jewell, Jane, 130
John Crerar Library, 89
Johns Hopkins University, 18, 99
Johnson, B. Lamar, 102
Johnson, Lyndon B., 55
Jones, Olive, 83
Jordan, Robert T., 54
Journal of Library and Information Science, 122, 124

Kai-ming Ch'iu, 115-16
Kai-tung Huang, Jack, 120
Kaser, David
    academic library publishing, 90
    biographical sketch, 129
    honors and achievements, 131-32
    library buildings, 120-22
    on library use instruction, 104
    Sino-American librarianship, 117-25

Kaufman, Paula, 19
Kennedy, James R., Jr., 105
Keogh, Andrew, 90, 92
Keys to access, Index, Table of contents, and the Title information (KITTs), 33, 35, 38
Kirk, Thomas, 103-4, 106
KITTs. *See* Keys to access, Index, Table of contents, and the Title information
Knapp, Patricia, 104
Koopman, H. L., 101
Korea, 122, 131
Krompart, Janet, 68
Kuo-chuin Liu, 116
Kuo-chun Chen, 119

Lafayette Papers Project, 130
Lai-lun Chau, 117
LAN. *See* Local area network
Land grant universities, 100
Lane, William C., 89
LCD. *See* Liquid crystal display screens
Lee, C. Y., 121
Leeds University, 70
Lewis, Harry F., 50
Library Association (United Kingdom), 69-70
Library Association of China, 117, 119
Library Binding Institute, 53
Library bindings, 52-53
Library buildings, 103, 120
    and computer technology, 13-28
"Library Development in Asia" (Kaser), 124
Library Development in Eight Asian Countries (Kaser), 124
"Library Development in the Republic of China" (Kaser), 124
"Library Educational Personnel Planning in ROC on Taiwan" (Mei-hua Yang), 118
Library expenditures, 38
Library Journal, 50, 82-83, 91, 97, 105
Library Literature, 105
Library of Congress Classification, 116
Library Planning and Media Technology (continuing education workshop), 119

Library professionals
  in China, 115-25
  education, 6-7, 9-12
  faculty status, 67-69, 71-75
  instructional positions, 105
  reference librarians, 86-87
  research and advanced study grants, 3-7
  United Kingdom certification, 69-71
Library Quarterly, 93
Library Resources and Technical Services, 131
"Library Resources for American Studies in Taiwan: An Evaluation" (Pin-chuan Chen), 118
Library schools
  in China, 115-16
  faculty positions, 9-10
  professional development programs, 6-7
  in Taiwan, 117
  in the United Kingdom, 71
Library Technology Project/Program (LTP), 49-50, 52, 60
Library use instruction, historical development, 97-106
Liquid crystal display (LCD) screens, 25
Little, Arthur D., Inc., 59
Little, George T., 83, 101
Local area network (LAN), 20
London, University of, 71
Louisiana State University, 7
Louttit, C. M., 102
LTP. *See* Library Technology Project/Program
"LTP—The Rattle in an Infant's Fist" (Clapp), 60

Macao, 122
Machine-readable books, 34. *See also* Electronic Information Delivery Online System (EIDOS)
Maddox, Lucy Jane, 82
Malaysia, 118
Management Intern programs of CLR, 8
Manchester University, 70
Manuscripts and Documents: Their Deterioration and Restoration (Barrow), 47
MARC records for online databases, 35
Martin, Susan K., 15, 18
Maryland, 9
McDonald, David, 18

McGraw-Hill Company, 123
Mei-hua Yang, 118
Meiklejohn, Alexander, 101
Mei Ya Publishing Company of Taipei, 122-23
Mellon, Andrew W., Foundation, 4
Memorial History of Boston (Winsor), 98
Messrs. Carey and Lea of Philadelphia (Kaser), 129
Michigan, 105
Michigan, University of, 7, 22, 86, 91, 130-31
Microfilm preservation and bibliographic control, 53-54
Mills College, 21, 23
Ming-chuan College, 120
Ming-hing Mok, 116
Minnesota, University of, 89
Missouri, 82, 131
Missouri Library Association Quarterly, 131
Monteith College, 104
Murray-Rust, Catherine, 17

Nanking, University of, 115-16
Narrative and Critical History of America (Winsor), 98
National Advisory Commission on Libraries, 55-56
National Central Library (NCL), 117-21, 132
National Cheng-chih University Library, 117
National Historical Publications Commission, 131
National Institute of the Arts, 119-21
National Library in Peiping, 116
National Microfilm Association, 54
National Palace Museum, 118
National Peking University, 116
National Register of Microform Masters (Library of Congress), 54
National Sun Yat-sen University, 116
National Taiwan Normal University, 119
National Taiwan University, 117, 119
National Union Catalog, 51, 56
NCL. *See* National Central Library
Nelson, C. Alex, 84
Newberry Library, 92
New England College Librarians' Association, 88

New York, 82, 94
New York Public Library, 14
New York Public Library School, 91
New York State Library, 90
New York State Library Association, 60, 101
Niagara Falls Conference of 1903, 85
Nigeria, 131
Notre Dame University, 131

Oberlin College, 101
OCLC. *See* Online Computer Library Center
Office of Management Studies (OMS), 6, 8
Ohio, 36
Ohio State University, 38, 83
Oklahoma, University of, 69-77
OMS. *See* Office of Management Studies
Online catalogs, noise factors, 21
Online Computer Library Center (OCLC), 14-15, 35-36. *See also* Electronic Information Delivery Online System
Online databases. *See* Electronic Information Delivery Online System
Online public access catalogs (OPAC), 18-19, 21, 23
OPAC. *See* Online public access catalog
Openability plate, 53
"Organizing an Oriental Collection" (Kaser), 124
Oxford University, 67-77

Pacific Cultural Foundation, 131
Pandolfo, Steven, 23
Paper preservation, 46-52, 56-60
Patrick, James, 102
Pau-sen Chen, 121
PC. *See* Personal computers
Peabody College, 117, 130
Pennsylvania, University of, 59, 99, 122
Pennsylvania State University, 21
"Perish the Paper, Perish the Book, Perish the Thought: An Inquiry" (Church), 47
"Permanence in Book Papers" (Barrow and Sproull), 47
"Permanence of Printing Papers" (GPO), 56
" 'Permanent/durable' Book Papers" (Clapp), 50

Permanent/durable paper project, 46-52, 56-60
Personal computers (PC), 22
PETREL. *See* Professional Education and Training for Research Librarianship
Pew Memorial Trust, 4
Phi Beta Kappa, 131
Philippines, 122
Phipp, Barbara, 102
Pin-chuan Chen, Robert, 118
"Plan for a Census of Library Resources" (Andrews), 89
"Plan for the Compilation of Comparative University and College Library Statistics" (Gerould), 89
Plum, Dorothy Alice, 90
Pocket Book of English Verse, 129
Pollack, Luella, 15
Poole, Frazer, 50, 52, 58
Power, Eugene, 54
Prabha, Chandra, 36
Prentice-Hall International, 124
Preservation of library materials, 45
  microfilm, 53-54
  paper, 46-52, 56-60
Preservation Research Office, 59
Princeton University, 89, 99, 115
Professional Education and Training for Research Librarianship (PETREL), 4, 6-8
"Proposed By-Laws of the College and Reference Section of A.L.A." (Goodrich), 91-92
Public Libraries in the United States, 88
Public Library Administrators' Planning Guide to Automation (Sager), 31
Publishers and publishing, book piracy, 122-24
Publisher's Weekly, 47

Q-decking, 17

Rader, Hannelore, 105
Ratcliffe, F. W., 69
Red Brick Universities, 70
Reed College, 15, 21, 23
Reference collections, 25
Reference librarianship, 86-87
Reference Librarians' Roundtable, 86
Regents of the State of New York, 82

Republic of China (ROC), 131-32
  Sino-American library activity, 115-25
Research grant support. *See* Grant
  programs
Research Libraries Group (RLG), 14
Research Libraries Information Network
  System, 15
Research Strategies, 105
Research Triangle Institute, 51
Restaurateur, 59
"Return of Cooperative Indexing"
  (Richardson), 89
Richardson, Ernest Cushing, 89-90, 99
RLG. *See* Research Libraries Group
ROC. *See* Republic of China
Root, Azariah Smith, 101
Rothstein, Samuel, 99
Rowell, Joseph C., 89
Rutgers University, 45

Sabine, Gordon A., 36
Sabine, Patricia L., 36
Sager, Donald, 31
St. Mary's College Library, 131
Saudi Arabia, 131
Science, 47
Security systems, 21
Se-Lin book-labeling device, 60
Seminar instruction, 99
Seminar on English Librarianship, 69
Seng, Harris B. H., 120
Senior Fellows program of CLR, 8
SGML. *See* Standard Generalized Markup
  Language
Shank, Russell, 23
Shaw, Ralph, 45
Sheffield University, 70
Shera, Jesse, 93
Shoemaker, Richard, 50
Shores, Louis, 101, 104
Short story indexes, 90
Siao-yuan Li, 116
Simonton, Wesley, 54
Simple Library Cataloging (Akers), 116
Singapore, 118
Sino-American library activity, 115
  classification systems, 116
  education and training of librarians,
    117-20
  joint understanding of books and
    libraries, 122-24

  library buildings, 120-22
  public library development, 116-17
  public services, 116
Sino-Japanese war, 117
Smart buildings, 26-27
Smith, Richard D., 59
Socrates online catalog, 18
Soletta, Chester, 130
Soviet Union, 103
Sproull, Reavis C., 47
Sputnik, 103
Standard Generalized Markup Language
  (SGML), 34-35
Stanford University, 15, 18-22
Stephens College, 102
Stewart, Nathaniel, 81
Stoffle, Carla, 105
"Story of Permanent/Durable Book Paper,
  1115-1970" (Clapp), 60
Stuart-Stubbs, Basil, 89
Study of How Books Are Used, 36
Subject Classification (Brown), 116
Sueling Li, 122
Sullivan, Laura, 68
Swanson, D. R., 33
*System of Book Classification for Chinese
  Libraries* (Kuo-chuin Liu), 116
*System of Classification of Chinese Books
  Based on Dewey's Classification*
  (Tsu-yung Seng), 116

Tables of contents, 31, 37
Taiwan. *See* Republic of China
Tauber, Maurice, 47
Teaching with Books (Branscomb), 102
Technical Services in Libraries (Tauber), 47
Telecommunications, 18
Telefacsimile machines, 22
Tennessee, 117, 130-31
Tennessee Library Association, 131
Texas, University of, 14, 23
"Trends and Issues in American
  Librarianship as Reflected in the
  Papers and Proceedings of the
  American Library Association,
  1876-1885" (Maddox), 82
Trinity College (Connecticut), 45
Trinity University, 70
Tsu-yung Seng, 116
Tung-li Yuan, 116-17, 119
Tun-sheng Hsiung, 123
Tze-chien Tai, 116

UCLA. *See* University of California at Los Angeles
Union List of Serials, 90, 99
Union lists, 89-90, 99
Union of Soviet Socialist Republics (USSR), 103
United Kingdom
 book industry, 122
 copyright law, 70
 faculty status of librarians, 67-77
 librarian certification, 69-71
U.S. Agency for International Development, 122
U.S. Bureau of Education, 88
U.S. Government Printing Office, 56
U.S. Library of Congress, 43, 52, 54-55, 58-60
U.S. Office of Education, 60
Universal book tester, 53
Universal catalog, 90
Universal Classification (Ding-u Doo), 116
University and College Librarians of the Mid-West, 88
University Convocations of the Regents of the State of New York, 82
University Library Associates Program, 7
University Microfilms, 54
University of Bristol, 67-77
University of British Columbia, 7
University of California at Berkeley, 17-18
University of California at Los Angeles (UCLA), 8, 17, 23
 Graduate School of Library and Information Science, 6
University of Chicago, 7, 59
University of London, library school, 71
University of Michigan, 7, 22, 86, 91, 130-31
University of Minnesota, 89
University of Nanking, 115-16
University of Notre Dame, 130
University of Oklahoma, 69
University of Pennsylvania, 59, 99
University of Pennsylvania Press, 122
University of Texas, 14, 23
University of Wellington (Canada), 38
University of Wisconsin, 7
"Use of the Library in Instruction" (Wilson), 102
Utley, George B., 92

Vaisey, David, 71, 74
Vanderbilt University, 117, 122, 130
Veysey, Laurence, 101
Vietnam, 131
Vi-line Wong, 116
Virginia, 45-46
Virginia State Library, 45, 47

Washington State University, 21
Washington University, 38
Washington University (St. Louis), 130
Wason Collection of Sinology, 118
Wee, Lily, 119
Wen-yu Yen, 116
Werrell, Emily, 68
Wesleyan University, 115
West Union University, 116
White Mountains Conference, 83
Who's Who Among Students in American Colleges and Universities, 130
Who's Who in America, 130
"Why Libraries Indeed?" (Kaser), 119
Widener Library, 15, 19. *See also* Harvard University
Williams, Gordon, 51, 59-60
Williams, Hugh, 90
Williams College, 22, 98
Wilson, Louis Round, 102
WilsonDisc services, 22
Winsor, Justin, 97-101, 106
Wisconsin, University of, 7
Wood, Mary Elizabeth, 115-16
World Anti-Communist League, 120
Wright, Louis, 54
Wuhan, China, 115
Wye Plantation, Maryland, 9

Yale University, 14, 90, 99
Yao-yu Bao, 121
Ying-hsuan Peng, 120
Yuan Tung-li Memorial Scholarship Fund, 119
Yu-feng Hung, 116
Yung-Hsiang Lai, 117